SELECTED GOLF COURSES

ɪF

BY HURDZAN•FRY

———

Photos and Essays Vol. 1

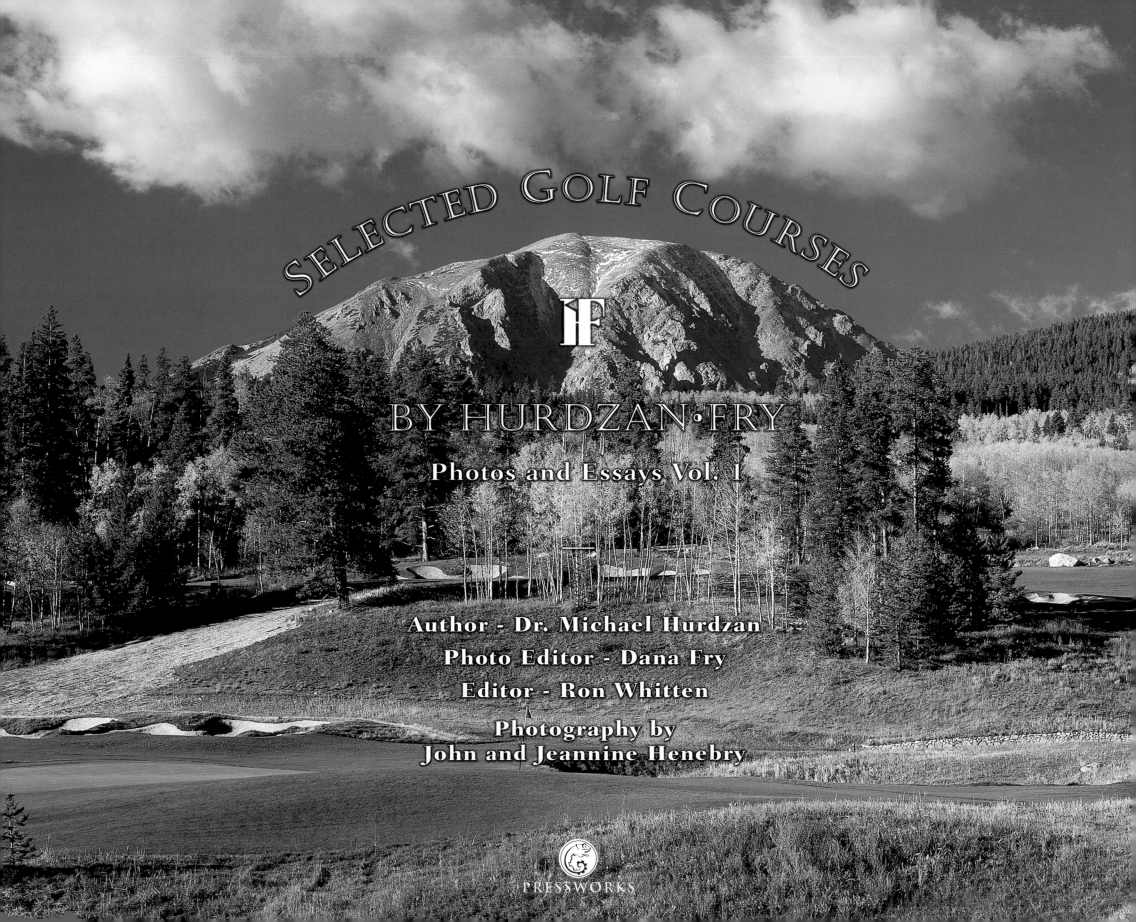

Selected Golf Courses

BY HURDZAN·FRY

Photos and Essays Vol. 1

Author - Dr. Michael Hurdzan

Photo Editor - Dana Fry

Editor - Ron Whitten

**Photography by
John and Jeannine Henebry**

PRESSWORKS

Hurdzan/Fry
Golf Course Design, Inc.
1270 Old Henderson Road
Columbus, Ohio 43220

Library of Congress Control Number: 2003100736
ISBN 0-9728553-0-0

Printed in U.S.A.
Photographers: John and Jeannine Henebry
Editor: Ron Whitten
Book Design: John Catania
Illustrations: Donald A. Keller
Printer: Pressworks, Inc.
First Edition:15,000
Publication Date: February 2003
384 Pages

DEDICATION

Jack Kidwell
(1917 - 2001)

Jack Kidwell was a humble man who loved people and the game of golf, and his skill at both was without peer. As a person, he lived a life of near-saintly proportions. He never had a bad word to say about anyone. He was sincerely interested in every person he met. He would make any sacrifice to help a friend.

Jack was a sharecropper's son who became an Ohio high school golf champion, an infantry officer in the Philippines, a loving husband, a devoted father and a treasure chest of thousands of loyal friends and fans. To simply meet Jack Kidwell was a significant moment for many people. For him to be part of your life was an even greater feeling.

As a golfer, he could be compared only to Old Tom Morris. Both were professional golfers (Jack was a Class A PGA member for many years), golf course superintendent (Jack was likewise a Class A superintendent), and golf course architect (Jack was president of the American Society of Golf Course Architects in 1980). His relevance to the Hurdzan/Fry family and alumni is incalculable. Not only was he the genesis of our firm in 1957, he was a mentor and second father to Mike and teacher and advisor to us all. His approach to golf and course design was simple and traditional, which explains why so few people are privileged to recognize his name and his work. His approach was purely functional, as he worked hard at keeping the cost of golf modest and the game available to all. His ideals led to millions of rounds of golf played on his 100 or so golf courses by every income level of golfer.

It is to a gentle man who inspired others by words and deeds that we dedicate this book.

TABLE OF CONTENTS

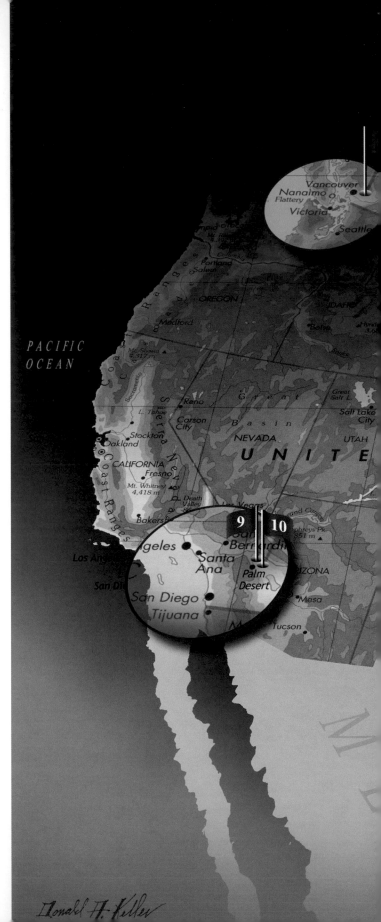

Donald H. Keller

PREFACE

*Michael Hurdzan
and Dana Fry*

There have been thousands of golf books dealing with nearly every facet of the game of golf, from Architecture to Zen. But I don't think I've ever read one that talked about the people, places and things that so strongly influence and mold a golf course into its final form. Like snowflakes, every single golf course has its own unique pattern. But its stories and circumstances are often lost with time. This book is my modest attempt to recall a few of the things that stand out about the Hurdzan/Fry course design projects highlighted in this book. I've chosen to write it in the first person, providing what I vividly remember about each project. I'm certain every person associated with each project will have different memories, perhaps even conflicting ones. This is not a record of cold hard facts. It's mostly impressions and recollections.

It was my partner Dana Fry's idea to have us produce a book featuring many of our golf designs. Dana wanted a pure photo book with very few words. Not that he's a person of few words (his enormous monthly cell phone bills prove otherwise). He just thought it would force people to study the photographs and discover the nuances of the holes, like people examining an Ansel Adams photo. But I thought just a bunch of pictures would be boring, and one golf course would blend into another. So we compromised, and this book is both photos and text.

We chose to work exclusively with the photography of the brother-and-sister team of John and Jeannine Henebry, because they are personal friends and because we think their photographs are incredible. Each will wait for hours for the right sun angle, or shadow or reflection or whatever they believe will capture the spirit and essence of each golf hole. This often means going back to a golf course several times for that one perfect shot. That may not be a cost-effective endeavor, but shooting golf courses is not just their livelihood, it's also their passion.

Ron Whitten, our longtime close friend (and Senior Architecture Editor for Golf Digest) once wrote that Dana and I are like "right brain, left brain." We always took that as a compliment (although we've never really asked Ron if it was intended that way), and it is a pretty good description. I tend to be the conservative technician, and Dana is much more the radical artist. We've had our fair share of disagreements, but we usually find a mutually acceptable compromise that allows us to act in a uniform way. This book is a good example.

Dana arranged for the photography in this book and selected all of the pictures. My job, was to do all of the writing. When we're done, we've agreed to review each other's contribution. So as I write this, I have no idea what photos Dana has selected, and he doesn't know what I've written about the courses. (I suspect Dana doesn't care, because he doesn't think anyone will read the text anyway). I am letting you know this so you can judge how harmoniously our partnership works, and to warn you that there may be little connection between written word and photographic visuals. So if you simply look at the pictures and read the captions, don't think you've read the entire book.

Publishing a book is a costly undertaking. Without the help and financial assistance of many of our friends and clients, this book couldn't have happened. Individual clubs arranged for the Henebry photography, but to publish this book we knew we'd have to find a money partner who believed in us and would trust us to repay him. That guardian angel is former client and lifetime friend Rick Hvizdak. Rick is avant-garde and finds appeal in zany projects like this. So here by the trust of Rick, and the grace of his checkbook, we are proud to present this book. For us, it's a family photo album sprinkled with reminders of people, places and things. We know it won't have the same effect on you, but we hope you'll find a bit of pleasure in learning about the genesis of some of the best golf courses designed by Hurdzan/Fry.

Michael J. Hurdzan

One of the great writers of his time, and certainly one of the best golf writers ever, Herbert Warren Wind in 1954 wrote the following:

"Ever since golf began-scottish historians have settled on the year 1100 as a reasonable date of birth-the game has been an enigma. For those who have steered clear of its clutches, the devotion it commands from its followers looms as one of the great absurdities of the human race's supposed progress. There are moments when every golfer agrees with this verdict.If he could only have back in one lump sum all the time, money, energy and anguish he has spent on golf and invest it toward some sensible goal, why, there is no knowing the heights of happiness he might reach. Then he plays a good round in congenial company on a sunny morning, and his golfers balance returns. If there is one thing he is certain he has done RIGHT in his life, it has been to play golf, and his only regret is that he hasn't given the game more time."

Having played the game for thirty five years both for fun and in competition, I can certainly attest to the truth of what Mr. Wind wrote. There is something about golf: once it has its grip on your soul, you are in for a life long relationship with a very fickle mistress. I have felt the exhilaration of holes-in-ones, holed bunker shots, 330 yard drives, and 80 foot putts that found the center of the cup. I have experienced the excitement of state amateur championships, collegiate golf, the PGA TOUR, Ryder Cups and Major Championships. I've won and I've lost. I've been in the final group four times on Sunday at the US Open without a victory, and have won the one I least expected to win: the British Open in 1996. But through the ups and the downs, the thrills and the disappointments, golf has always had its way with me. It has always been more than a game; it has been a way of life.

Grantland Rice wrote in 1926 "Golf is, in part, a game; but only in part. It is also in part a religion, a fever, a vice, a mirage, a frenzy, a fear, an abscess, a joy, a thrill, a pest, a disease, an uplift, a brooding melancholy, a dream of yesterday, a disappointing today, and a hope for tomorrow." Golf always keeps me coming back. There is always more that I want to achieve and eternally a desire to improve. The great thing about the game for me is that I can have just as much fun playing for pride with my family and friends as I can playing at Augusta in the Masters. It's because once golf is in your soul, you just want to be around it, to play it, to watch it, to talk about it, and whether the stakes are very high or there are none at all, the game remains unconquerable.

No game tests the human spirit nor defines our character like the game of golf. Nearly every emotion known to man can be felt at some time during any normal single round of golf. The other main reason for my love of golf is the beauty of the game. There is a rhythm and balance and flow to golf, this is true, and to watch someone who is good at it is definitely something to behold. But the beauty that I am talking about is the literal beauty of the golf course: The different shades of green, the shadows as the sun rises and sets, the gold, orange and red leaves on the green grass in the fall, the rolling contours of the fairways, the balance created by well placed bunkers, the contrast of tan fescue grass against the green of the roughs and fairways, the mirror-like look of a pond when the wind is non-existent.........the list could go on and on. To me, the beauty of a golf course stirs my soul.

I can remember standing on the 7th fairway at Pinehurst #2 during the Tour Championship in October of 1992 and just being overwhelmed with the tranquility, harmony and serenity of the setting. It was one of those peak moments in life that I will never forget and as I think back on it, it was because of the perfect blending of golf and nature. That was what evoked such strong emotions within me. That golf course looked like it has been there since the beginning of time and it seemed that God, not Donald Ross, has just laid 18 holes upon the pine treed sand belt of North Carolina. That day has influenced me more than anyone will ever know.

George Thomas, the famed designer during the golden age of golf course design, once said that, "To my mind, the most important thing in the championship course is the terrain, because no matter how skillfully one may lay out the holes and diversify them, nevertheless one must get the trill of nature." Lyle Anderson, a friend who happens to also be very successful in the golf development business, once gave me the advice that if I want to be known as a great designer, then "only take projects with great pieces of land." All of the courses that we hold in such high regard today were built on phenomenal pieces of ground. Nature is what makes or breaks the eternal quality of the golf experience, and it is up to the architect to use it wisely and wonderfully. And that brings me to the point of this entire exercise, and that is to say, how much I admire and respect Dr. Mike Hurdzan and Dana Fry in their pursuit of just such a purpose.

These men don't often have the luxury to choose or reject their projects based on how good the terrain. Instead, they are talented, experienced designers who can take mundane topography and give it a unique natural character, or a great site and ensure that the golf features compliment and not compete with nature. They can work with both exiting environments, or create fresh functional ones, but all of their golf courses are playable, maintainable, and sustainable. I can honestly say there is no human on this earth who has more passion for golf course design than either Mike or Dana. They may be tied, but they can't be surpassed. I have spent a lot of time with both in the course of the work we did together at Troy Burne and at the Raven at Three Peaks. They understand the responsibility to the game and to the projects that they have. They are great caretakers of the traditions of golf.

Besides the stunning photography of John and Jeannine Henebry, and the insightful captions that accompany them, there are the stories behind the golf courses that rarely ever get told, except by publicists or ad agencies. Mike and Dana care as much about people as they do their work and the stories of each golf course will show that. There never has been a golf book quite like this, but then again there have not been many design teams quite like Mike and Dana. Of all the people whom I have met in golf, there are none that I enjoy being around more or whom I respect more than Mike Hurdzan and Dana Fry. Golf is filled with people like these two, and I feel just as strongly about every one of them as well. I mean, Jack Nicklaus is just an incredible person and competitor and I respect him a great deal. For not only the kind of people they are, but also for what they do in their own professional pursuit of perfection in golf course design. I regard Mike and Dana just as highly. Need I say more?

Only this: I'm proud to call them friends.

Tom Lehman
January 1, 2003

Michael Hurdzan, ASGCA
Principal

Dr. Michael Hurdzan winner of the 2002 Donald A. Rossi Award from the Golf Course Builders Association of America; has also been named Golf World Magazine's "Architect of the Year;" and twice The Board Room Magazine's selection for the same honor. Dr. Hurdzan is an internationally recognized authority on golf course environmental issues. He teaches "Environmental Impacts of Golf Courses" for the Harvard Graduate School of Design. He is a Golf Digest/GCSAA panelist for their environmental awards program, a selected delegate for the "Golf and Environment" conferences, and serves as a trustee for the Environmental Institute on Golf. Mike is a past president of the American Society of Golf Course Architects, and his 400-page book on golf course architecture has been called "the modern bible of golf course design."

Dana Fry, ASGCA
Principal

Dana Fry has worked with Dr. Michael Hurdzan since 1988, and became a full partner in 1997. He is a member of the American Society of Golf Course Architects, and a past member of its Board of Directors. Golfweek magazine selected Dana among the TOP FIVE in their 2001 "40 under 40" list of people in leadership positions within the golf industry who are likely to shape the business for years to come. Dana learned his craft working as a field designer for Tom Fazio, and was instrumental in the creation of several award-winning courses for the Fazio organization. No one is more passionate about the profession than Dana.

David Whelchel, ASGCA
Senior Design Associate

David Whelchel has been with Hurdzan/Fry since 1990 and serves as the Senior Project Design Manager in all phases of various projects. Whelchel is an agriculture graduate from the University of Arkansas where he also served as men's golf coach before becoming involved with golf course construction and subsequently design. David is a member of the American Society of Golf Course Architects, Golf Course Superintendents Association of America, Golf Collectors Society, and the USGA. He has traveled extensively and has studied golf courses around the world including over 500 courses played and many more visited.

Bill Kerman, ASGCA
Senior Design Associate

Bill Kerman is a civil engineer by training, a golf course architect by choice. With his extensive technical background, he specializes in projects with severe site and environmental restrictions. Due to his engineering background, Bill is well versed in the land planning and development process. He is proficient in integrating the difficult, and often conflicting, demands of combined development / golf projects. Bill is a registered Professional Engineer. He is also a member of the American Society of Golf Course Architects and the Golf Course Superintendents Association of America. Bill has been with Hurdzan/Fry Design since 1989.

Jason Straka
Senior Design Associate

Jason Straka joined Hurdzan/Fry Design in October of 1995. Straka has been trained in many aspects of golf course architecture, however he specializes in environmental design. He earned a Bachelors degree in landscape architecture and a Masters degree in environmental golf course design studies, both from Cornell University. Jason's primary university work was on the development of Widow's Walk Golf Course in Scituate Massachusetts, which is widely recognized as the United State's first environmental demonstration and research golf course, and winner of GOLF DIGEST'S prestigious "Environmental Leaders in Golf" award. Straka is a member of the Golf Course Superintendents Association of America.

Scott Kinslow
CAD Technician

Scott Kinslow is Senior Computer Design Technician and has been with Hurdzan/Fry since 1988. He specializes in computer aided design and drafting and develops innovative ways to program software packages to produce more descriptive and accurate plans and specifications. In addition, Scott has had extensive experience in the building trades and brings with him management and organizational skills that ensure complete construction documentation.

Christopher Hurdzan
Design Associate

Chris Hurdzan has worked in the business on a part-time basis since high school. He attends The Ohio State University on a full-time career path to golf course design. Although young, he is learning every aspect of the craft from the most skilled of practitioners. His college work in an environmental science program adds to the diversity of backgrounds and skills found at Hurdzan/Fry. Chris has also worked in golf course construction, and maintenance.

Robert Grossi
Director of Marketing

Bob Grossi is Director of Marketing, Video, and Public Relations for Hurdzan/Fry Golf Course Design. He has over 20 years experience as a radio and television writer, producer, moderator, narrator, and journalist. Bob has directed the marketing, and public relations efforts of Hurdzan/Fry since 1992. In addition to his regular duties of marketing the services of H/F, he also consults with clients of the firm and in some cases even provides practical assistance with their marketing and membership programs. Bob is an avid golfer and offers the designers his critical perspectives. He was responsible for coordinating all the elements of this book.

P.J. Barton and Linda Hurdzan
Administrative Coordinators

P.J. and Linda are two of the hardest working and talented office managers that any office could have. At Hurdzan/Fry they are the first people to greet you and from then on comes a commitment to seeing that our client's concerns are always addressed. Given the hectic travel schedule of the designers, it becomes P.J. and Linda who can always track down answers or a designer to satisfy client requests. Their efficient day-to-day office management means each of the designers can focus on his area of specialization, while P.J. & Linda cover all of the necessities of running a business.

Portraits by Will Shiveley

Rick Hvizdak - Financial backing

Rick Hvizdak is first and foremost a best friend, with whom we have enjoyed sharing thousands of hours designing his golf course, playing golf courses everywhere, and just being social. He is a man of his word as much as he is a man of means. Without his trust, patience and help, this book would still just be our dream.

Ron Whitten - Editor

Ron Whitten, now Senior Editor, Architecture for Golf Digest magazine, has written about golf course design for over 25 years, including four books on the subject. He boasts the unofficial world's record for playing courses with their architects, but is even more proud about collaborating with Hurdzan/Fry on the design of a new course in Wisconsin.

Vince Simone - Project Manager/Printing

Vince Simone of Pressworks Inc., is a thirty-five year veteran of the Printing and Graphic Arts Industry. His work has won numerous awards. Besides being a long time avid golfer, he readily identifies with many of the personalities portrayed in this book, as he was instrumental in the building of Hickory Hills, a private golf club near Columbus, Ohio, with Jack Kidwell and Mike Hurdzan in 1977. As one of the original founders, he continues to serve on the Board of Directors, and the Green Committee to this day.

John Catania - Book Design

John is the Studio Director at Gerbig Snell/Weisheimer & Associates, Inc. He manages a group called "The Studio" which is a creative group specializing in Graphic Design.

Donald A. Keller - Routing Plan Illustrations

Don is a highly acclaimed medical/surgical illustrator, whose specialty is illustrating surgical procedures in ophthalmology. The hallmark of his illustration technique is seemingly infinite detail and extreme precision. He regards golf courses as the ideal subject... an opportunity to apply his disciplined approach to illustrating.

Steve Chappelear - Color Imaging Consultant

Steve is Vice President of Cardinal Imaging, Inc., Columbus, OH. He provided the color separations and image retouching on this project.

DEVIL'S PULPIT

The board game Trivial Pursuit® is the second largest selling game in the world, behind the much older game of Monopoly. It was invented in the 1970s by two low-paid newspaper guys who, one evening, while debating whether to buy a SCRABBLE® game or spend their last few dollars on more beer, decided to invent their own board game. The rest, as the saying goes, is history. Trivial Pursuit® made its creators, Chris Haney and Scott Abbott, very wealthy guys. Wealthy guys often become golf nuts, and golf course owners.

According to lore, Chris was at one of his favorite watering holes complaining how he was unable to get a tee time at his local club, when someone suggested that he build his own golf course. To most sane people, this would have been good for a laugh. But for Chris, it became a not-so-Trivial Pursuit® that culminated in not one, but two, of the best golf courses in the world.

The opening hole at any course should set the character for the holes that follow. The Pulpit's 1st hole offers golfers at least four options on how to play its 478 yards. Short hitters play to the left fairway, longer hitters can go left of the tree, long knockers can go right of the tree and pros can aim for the right fairway. The payoff is that the farther right one plays, the shorter this par 4 becomes. This is pure risk and reward.

Canadian Chris Haney is not only a guy with a wonderful sense of humor, but also enormous vision, persuasion and determination. He's very methodical, but he places great trust in his instincts and he is rarely wrong. Chris hired me after we'd spent several hours together at his home. He did so without ever having heard of me, or playing one of my courses, or even seeing a picture of a golf hole I designed. "I want you to design me a world class golf course," he said, "and I know you can do it."

Many believe that the 12th hole is the best par 4 on the course. The most open approach to its 423-yard demanding green is from the left edge of the fairway on the dogleg left hole. But to reach that landing area short of the left fairway bunker takes a long, accurate drive that must carry a hollow of rough covered in thick bluegrass. Bailout is as far right as one wants to go.

Usually a tree in the middle of a fairway is hokey. Here on the 10th hole, the tree is so perfectly shaped and located that it makes the hole special without being unfair. Most drives land near the base of the tree, but even on a short drive there is always room for a second shot either left or right of the tree.

Prior to this, I was the king of B-movies, designer of cheap but functional golf courses that barely got recognition in my hometown, let alone the world. But I knew, given the chance, I could do a world-class course, and so Chris and I set off on our mission.

I suggested to Chris that the best way to get a great golf course is to begin with a great site. A few weeks later he and I, along with others, spent time evaluating countless sites. I ranked them in order from best to worst. Chris and Scott bought the 300 acres that was my number one choice. I was awed by the beauty of the land and excited by the possibilities of 300 acres for nothing but golf. Chris's only stipulation was where the clubhouse had to go, atop a hill with views into downtown Toronto 35 miles away. The only problem with Chris's clubhouse site was it made getting return nines almost impossible. After much planning, I came to the conclusion the only way to make his clubhouse work was to buy 15 more acres, land where the ninth hole is today.

He and Scott had every intention of buying the extra land from the moment I mentioned it, but they enjoyed stringing me along for a time. "I gave you 300 acres for one lousy 18-hole golf course, with no housing," Chris said mockingly, "and you tell me now I need more land!" Well, yes. There aren't too many world-class 17-hole golf courses in the world.

The additional land allowed us to create what is perhaps the greatest starting hole in golf. The back tee of the first hole at the Pulpit is at nearly the same elevation as the top of CN Tower in downtown Toronto, which is a good target point for a drive that drops 90 feet to a double fairway on this long par 4.

The 7th hole has nine separate tees and its longest possible yardage is 132 yards. However, do not let the short length fool you, for the green sits up on top of a knob and the wind is a big factor. At times one must start the ball well off the green and allow the wind to bring it home. In addition, target areas within the green are generous but not forgiving. This is one tough short hole.

A long 445-yard par 4 that plays uphill, and often into the wind, doesn't sound like much fun, but the 4th hole somehow manages it. Perhaps it is just the wide variety of colors, textures and heights that define the golf hole. Or it may be the wide fairway and equally wide open approach into the green that encourages an aggressive golf swing without fear of hazards. Whatever the reason, this hole is fun to play.

That was a difficult hole to build. And an expensive one. Chris still shakes his head when he says, "I hired this guy who used to build entire golf courses for a million dollars, and this first hole alone cost us $1.3 million." And it's true, but no one can step onto the first tee without saying something like, "Oh, my God. Look at that!"

Devil's Pulpit was my breakthrough project, for it won Golf Digest's Best New Canadian golf course award in 1990 and was followed two years later by sister course Devil's Paintbrush. But just as important as that project was for my career, it was perhaps more important that during this time I met Dana Fry.

Devil's Pulpit

Caledon Village, Ontario, Canada

HOLE	PAR	YDS
1	4	478
2	4	364
3	3	182
4	4	445
5	4	401
6	4	415
7	3	132
8	5	485
9	4	401
OUT	35	3303
10	4	413
11	4	459
12	4	423
13	5	512
14	4	425
15	4	438
16	3	230
17	4	456
18	4	493
IN	36	3849
TOTAL	71	7152

I knew that I was a good technician, but I was not an artist, and for the Pulpit to be one of the best in the world, I needed help. I bumped into my good friends Pete and Alice Dye at the annual conference and show of the Golf Course Superintendent's Association of America. Trailing them like a devoted puppy was Dana, who had just finished five years as a shaper with Tom Fazio, having worked on 16 of Tom's projects. Dana was ready to move on and had Pete and Alice in his sights. Perhaps in an effort to shake this kid, Alice said to me, "Mike, here's a young guy I think you should meet."

This photo of the 8th hole does a nice job capturing the beauty of the hole, but not its strategy, which few photos can ever do. The par 5 is 485 yards long, and after an aggressive tee shot, golfers can choose to play directly at the green with a long uphill shot to a narrow opening, or bail out to an upper right fairway or a lower left one. An elevation difference of eight feet separates the fairway, along with several bunkers cut into the face between the two.

The par-3 3rd has a huge green that seems impossible to miss on a hole only 182 yards long. However, such a big green allows for some very bold contours to define target areas within the green. Believe it or not, the easiest hole locations are near the right front bunker and in the left rear of the green, which is a couple of feet lower and 30 yards farther back. The hole location shown here requires flirting with the tree on the left, but is still easy to reach. The toughest hole location is right rear.

When construction began on the Pulpit, Dana moved up with his young family into an extra house Scott Abbott had on his property. In addition, I hired a young man by the name of Guy Quattrocchi who had just finished a stint doing construction for Perry Dye (the older son of Pete and Alice), so he also lived on the job. Over the years, Dana and Guy would work together on Devil's Pulpit, Devil's Paintbrush, both courses at Desert Willow and several others in this book. The standard joke in our office became, "I provide the vision. They provide the product." We became a strong team that plays to each other's strengths. They come up with fantastic, artistic ideas. I get stuck solving all the problems to make the ideas work.

This is a rather unusual view of the 11th hole, as there are no tees back here, but perhaps there should be. The forward tee is in the foreground from which a drive must carry only 20-25 yards of native grass to reach the wide, wide fairway on this 459-yard long par 4. The other tees are set progressively further to the left, and from the back tee the drive must carry the deep fairway bunker on the left. Choose your tee and your pleasure.

A few more words about Chris Haney. We had budgeted for about 20 acres of sod for the Pulpit, which was an unusually large sod order for a golf course back then. Once the sod started going down, Chris decided he wanted the whole place sodded. Before long, we had used almost 100 acres of sod. This was such hot, strenuous, dirty work that Chris felt sorry for the laborers. So he had a swimming pool installed, so they'd have something to look forward to at the end of each long day. To this day, Chris Haney is Dana's number one cult figure hero.

Dana and I admit to extreme prejudice about Devil's Pulpit and its sister Devil's Paintbrush, but I challenge anyone to show me a 36-hole club that offers as much beauty, diversity, excitement, great golf and good natured people than the Devil's Pulpit Golf Association. They are arguably the best courses in Canada, courses that are making history.

The 1st hole gave golfers optional fairways and very distinct landing areas. The par-4 2nd has only one fairway, but is only 364 yards long, so it can be played with a short safe drive that leaves a 7-iron or less to the green, or it can be attacked with a driver to leave a short wedge shot approach. The difference is the margin of error allowed for each strategy. The longer the drive, the greater the intensity of hazard. It's a different form of risk and reward.

When asked which is their favorite golf course, most golf course architects dodge the question by saying, "That is like asking me to say which is my favorite child." Well, I don't dodge the question. Devil's Paintbrush is my favorite child, and my favorite course to play. It is as close to a true links golf course as can be built on inland land. The only difference is that the sand dunes beneath the golf course were formed by a glacier 10,000 years ago instead of by wind and waves. The randomness of its contours, with humps and hollows that defy the natural forces of water erosion, are the same as a seaside links. The combination of porous sandy soils and constant drying winds usually limit vegetation to low growing prairie and pasture grasses. But when these same soils are planted to the fine fescue grasses common to European seaside links, and are given an occasional irrigation, they produce a dry, fast surface and capricious bounce and roll that is the heart and soul of links golf. I don't believe there are but a handful of true links golf experiences in North America, and Devil's Paintbrush is one of the best.

———————————

If there is a true links hole in North America, this is it. From the regular tees, the 10th hole plays 352 yards across the entrance drive to the club, over and between stacked stone walls, to a wide fescue fairway peppered with sod wall pot bunkers, and then a blind shot to an uphill green. Folks who play and enjoy European links golf love this hole. But love it or hate it, this short par 4 rewards smart golf shotmaking.

Just as the 1st hole at the Pulpit sets the character of that golf course, so does this opening hole at the Paintbrush - and they are two distinctly different characters. While the Pulpit is North American bentgrass elegance, the Paintbrush is European fine fescue naturalness. Both have wide fairways but on the Paintbrush you must worry about hidden hazards, great flowing bunkers, in-play stone walls and grasses left to grow in an unmaintained way. Both require strategic thinking, but the Paintbrush puts more emphasis on it.

From any tee this is a driveable par 4 of 293 yards, if you choose the right line. Clearly the bold line is directly at the left green bunker but a mishit may end up in a cross-bunker, or worse yet in the only tree on the hole, the little hawthorn. There are many smart ways to play this 3rd hole, but most golfers pull out the driver and go for the green. As you can imagine, the green has its own devilish character, so most people are satisfied with a par.

All of its bunkers have stacked sod faces. Water only comes into play on two holes. Fairways are twice as wide as on average golf courses. Blind shots are celebrated not cursed. Undulations of four to five feet in a green are not unusual. An endless supply of dry-stacked stone walls give the appearance of a giant maze. Golfers not only hit shots at the Paintbrush, they must invent some, like a putter from 50 yards off the green or a lob wedge over a pot bunker from a tight lie. Only four or five trees were removed to build the golf course, and 90 per cent of the required earthmoving occurred on two holes, just to get rid of dirt generated from digging the irrigation pond.

Dana and I love playing European linksland golf, especially in Ireland where white guide rocks help golfers aim blind shots. At the 5th hole, the drive is into a bowl shaped fairway that is nearly impossible to miss, but it will leave a blind shot to the green, visible in this picture. There are three guide rocks to help aim your approach, ones designating the right and left edges and middle of the green. Once you hit your second, there is delayed gratification until you climb the ridge and see where your ball ended up. Many shots land short, catch the slope and roll onto the green. Really bad shots are bunkered.

The essence of playing golf at Devil's Paintbrush is to understand what the mythical Shivas Irons talked about in the book Golf In The Kingdom. It's true gravity coupled with the confounding influence of ever changing winds. To play the course well means having a diverse set of skills, great imagination and good karma. To play the golf course well two days in a row means having a good bit of luck, for the course plays very differently each day. On those days when intense concentration on golf is not on the agenda, the Paintbrush can fill your mind with changing patterns of color, texture and light, and provide visual images that stir some ancient hardwired sense of peace and tranquility. It is a magical place, where you can play a special brand of golf, and feel like every discretionary minute invested there was a wise choice.

The flagstick looks real short on this par 3 16th. Well, the flagstick is a full seven feet tall, so that indicates the right side of the green behind the bunker is five feet lower than the left side. This was the natural contour we found, so we left it. It now makes the shot to either side of the green more fun. Most hole-in-ones happen on the right hole location. You just can't see it - so you hope.

If there is any better par 5 on this continent, I haven't seen it. The 8th hole plays at 574 yards from the back tee to a 100-yard wide fairway that flows around a historic barn foundation and watering trough that is directly in the landing area. Most drives easily avoid the ruins, leaving a second shot that should carry the world's largest and highest sod wall bunker (70 yards long and up to 16 feet deep). Reaching the green in two is rare because of a deep grassy hollow in front of the small green. The backdrop is the city of Toronto, 35 miles away.

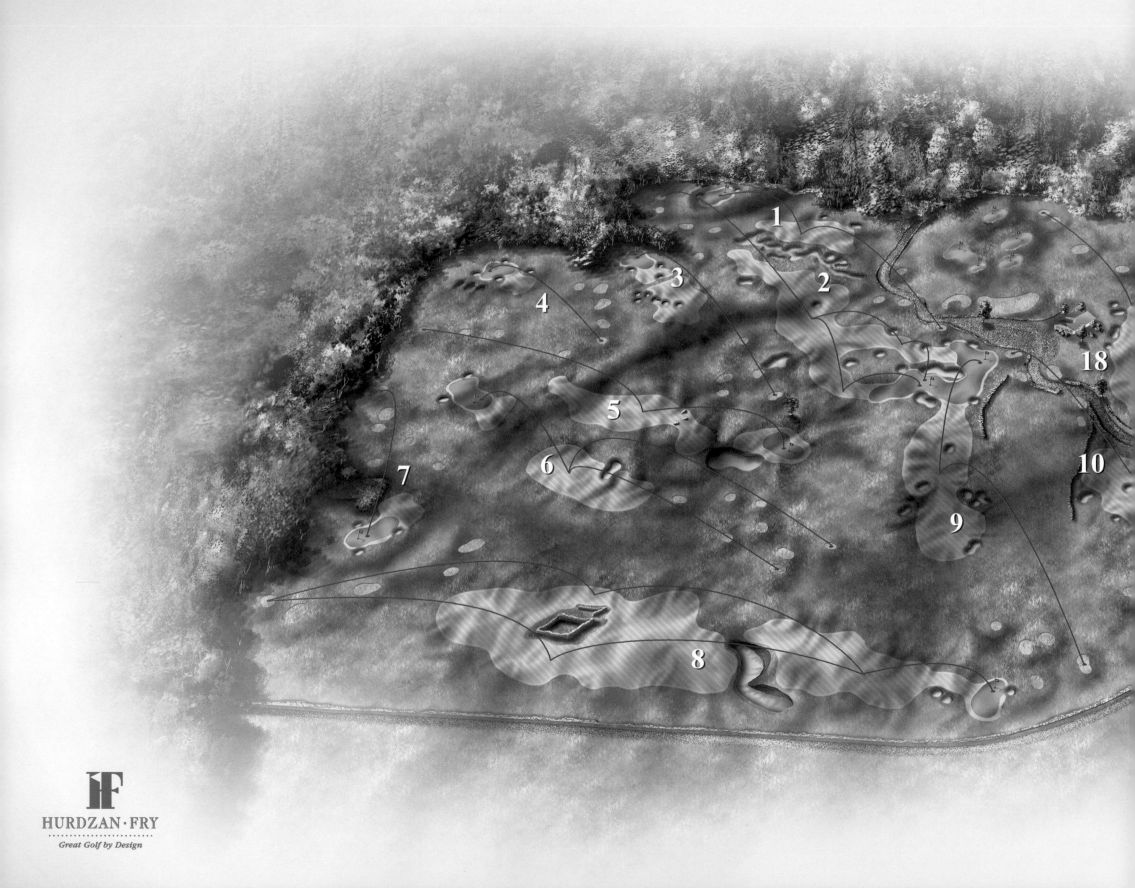

Devil's Paintbrush

Caledon East, Ontario, Canada

©2002 Donald H. Keller

HOLE	PAR	YDS	HOLE	PAR	YDS
1	4	371	10	4	352
2	5	468	11	5	591
3	4	293	12	4	394
4	3	191	13	3	226
5	4	428	14	5	548
6	4	419	15	4	372
7	3	202	16	3	159
8	5	574	17	4	413
9	4	383	18	4	388
OUT	36	3329	IN	36	3443
			TOTAL	72	6772

The 388-yard 18th ends the round as spectacularly as the first hole starts it, but for different reasons. Although 18 has lots of undulation in the fairway, the main complicating factor is the front left green bunker. It is about 10 feet deep at the far end with a sheer sod wall face. There is plenty of room all around this formidable hazard, but it seems like at least one ball per foursome finds it.

There is only one pond on the course and it is mainly there to store irrigation water. But it is also a strategic hazard on the par-4 15th. This view taken from the tee shows how early evening shadows hide the key driving bunkers on the left side of the fairway. The land slopes to the right, so a proper tee shot is directly at the left bunkers to allow it to run to the center of the fairway, setting up a short pitch across the pond.

iF
37

Without question, there is a spiritual quality to The Paintbrush. It is not a demon's tool. (The real Devil's Paintbrush, by the way, is a yellow and red wildflower that grows on the site). The natural spirit of the place seems to connect well to the human spirit...and to liquid spirits. The clubhouse (called Professor Rabbit's Hole by one of the founders, Scott Abbott) consists mainly of an Irish pub. The only things on the menu are Irish -- bangers and mash, shepherd's pie, Irish stew and the like -- except for the wide variety of European distillates served in the rose garden behind the clubhouse, an enclave some 20 feet above and adjacent to the landing zone on the closing hole. From that quiet spot you can see the skyline of Toronto 35 miles to the south and nearly all of the countryside in between, including the entire 17th and 18th holes. You can watch golfers play every stroke on those two holes, even shots out of a couple of 10-foot-deep bunkers. I once suggested to co-founder Chris Haney that he should hide a microphone in one of those bunkers and put speakers in the rose garden, so we can attach words to the emotional gyrations we see when golfers struggle to extricate a ball.

⊰ There are not many places in North America where one must play directly over stone walls, but you do at the 413-yard 17th. The wall crosses the fairway about 160 yards from the middle tee, so it really is more of a psychological than real hazard, but taken together with the native grass rough, sod-wall bunkers and an undulating fairway, it makes it memorable. If variety is the spice of life, this golf course is gourmet rich in spice and life.

The golf holes at The Paintbrush are actually manmade, but were done with such naturalness that it looks like the holes just happened and we simply added bunkers. At Devil's Paintbrush, we may have achieved the artistic goal of hiding the art.

The problem with all photos of golf holes is that they fail to show the intensity of slopes that golfers see and measure with their eyes and brains to select and execute golf shots. For instance, this view of the tee shot on the par-3 7th looks pretty mundane, but in person, you'd see the huge left to right slope of this entire complex that shrinks your choices down to aiming more towards the left bunker or praying. The hardest hole locations are far right.

Annbriar
GOLF COURSE

It didn't start out that way, but Annbriar Golf Course was built as a tribute for Ann Nobbe, the daughter of owners William and Nancy Nobbe. Ann was a talented and gifted woman who died at age 26, far too young. Before her death in an auto accident, she had a promising career in real estate and had encouraged her parents to join two of their favorite things together - the family farm and the game of golf.

We had begun schematic designs prior to Ann's accident. After the accident, the Nobbe family was so shaken that all planning stopped. Several months later, William called and told us that he, Nancy, and their two other children, Dan and Russ, had decided to proceed with the course that Ann had been so enthusiastic about, and dedicate it to her memory.

William Nobbe is a big, strong man who'd worked hard all of his life, and he wanted to be part of the actual construction process. No job was too tough, too complicated or too menial for William. He tried to do it all, as his efforts were for Ann. One of our fondest memories is seeing William driving a loaded monster dump truck up and down hills so steep we were afraid to drive a four-wheeler over them.

One of our associates, Guy Quattrocchi, lived on the project and directed construction on a day-to-day basis. Alois Lohr, a tough old Missouri contractor who became the Nobbes' partner, thought he could build the course without the help of any golf course construction company, but as time went on, he developed a respect for the construction crew. We still see Alois at our annual golf outings and he still refers to Joe Niebur, of Niebur Golf Course Construction, as "that kid."

The 13th hole is a 383-yard par 4 that requires a drive across a deep ravine to a wide, flat fairway. From that generous fairway, the approach shot is across a natural drainage swale about 10 feet deep to an equally generous green. Like most of our greens we design in about 75% easy hole locations and four to five competitive, hard-to-attack locations. It should be obvious the hard hole locations are on the back shelf.

The 8th hole plays downhill for 426 yards, through a manmade valley that allows the wide fairway to meander, creating a pleasant mixture of colors and textures. The green is narrow, with hazards on the left but only the steep hillside on the right. This hole has nearly perfect visual balance.

Annbriar was one of Dana's favorite projects and the Nobbes one of his favorite families. Each week, when he visited the job, he'd stay with the Nobbes in their big farmhouse on the property. Nancy would have his favorite potato chips on hand, and would make him chocolate chip cookies without nuts. William once remarked he'd be glad when the project was finished and Dana wouldn't visit as often, so Nancy could start putting nuts back in the cookies again. Even today, Dana takes his entire family by for a visit to the Nobbe family farm for a day or two.

Unlike the humpy, bumpy fad of the 1970s and 1980s of funky-looking mounds, today's golf course shaping is subtle and soft. Rather than building mounds for backdrops to greens, our preference is for naturalness, like trees and the rustic-looking fence, beyond this green complex on the 5th hole.

The panorama from behind the 7th green shows all of the textures on this golf course. There is the velvety smoothness of the putting surface that gives way to lighter colored and more coarse grasses used on fairways, which in turn are framed by taller, darker green rough grasses. Beyond that are the wetland plants found along pond edges, woods and stone walls and a final backdrop of blue skies. It is no wonder that golfers enjoy the naturalness of a golf course.

HOLE	PAR	YDS	HOLE	PAR	YDS
1	4	361	10	4	408
2	4	435	11	4	404
3	4	385	12	4	368
4	3	193	13	4	383
5	5	514	14	5	509
6	4	388	15	3	172
7	3	165	16	4	466
8	4	426	17	3	166
9	5	495	18	5	603
OUT	36	3362	IN	36	3479
			TOTAL	72	6841

Annbriar
Waterloo, Illinois

15

18

14

13

12

10

11

©2002 Donald F. Keller

HURDZAN·FRY
Great Golf by Design

Sometimes you can walk on a site and find a perfectly natural golf hole. At Annbriar, it was the 404-yard par-4 11th. From the tees elevated 30 feet above the fairway, you can see the double dogleg fairway that has the creek first on the left, then across the middle and finally along the right side of the green. The hole is perfectly framed by trees and this valley is so quiet and isolated that even bird songs sound loud.

The Nobbe property was a dramatic collage of topographical features including rolling farm fields, steep hills, rock cliffs, ravines, magnificent trees, ponds, waterfalls and little creeks that became mighty during rainstorms. The golf holes we produced on this land are no less dramatic. The fifth hole started life as a flat cornfield, but after many thousands of yards of earthmoving, it became an undulating fairway bordered by rolling hills on the left and an enlarged farm pond on the right (see photo). The 11th plays down through a meandering valley, flanked by great trees and bisected by a bubbling brook with the green perched on its bank. The home hole, plays through a natural valley that terminates below the clubhouse.

≺ *Sometimes what appears to be a very natural golf hole is really the result of a heck of a lot of construction. Such was the case on the 14th, where the valley was too narrow and poorly drained, there was no green site to speak of, and we had to protect a small creek that flowed through the area. Back 50 years ago, this would have been an impossible hole to build, but with modern construction equipment it was only a matter of time and money to get the 509-yard par 5 hole to fit right.*

Steep terrain lends itself best to par 3 holes, especially when two hilltops are separated by only 166 yards and a deep valley, like at the 17th hole. Basically, Dana shaped in tees on one hillside, cut a green into another one, and then redirected a natural swale to become a recirculating waterfall. The right side bunker is for visual balance. Very few shots end up there.

When you visit Annbriar, you'll likely meet William and Nancy, for they are always there, still working hard to make each round a special golf experience. You'll feel the warmth of a family kindled by their love for Ann and sustained by her memory. There is a purity about Annbriar that is rare and absorbing, as well as a great place to play golf.

───────────

≺ *As much care is taken in designing finish holes as opening holes, because a golf course should start and finish strong. The par-5 603-yard 18th is definitely a strong finisher. It begins with a downhill drive across a small, natural, spring-fed pond to a narrow bowl-shaped fairway. The second shot is slightly downhill and the third shot is uphill to a green cut into a hillside just below the clubhouse dining room. Whether playing the hole or just relaxing and watching others play it, it is memorable.*

No golfer is especially fond of water hazards, but they can add a great deal of variety, interest and strategy to what would otherwise be a bland hole. Still, it takes skillful placement of such hazards by the designer. The original site for the 5th hole was a flattish cornfield with a small farm pond that was a perfect candidate to be greatly enlarged, both as a hazard and to provide fill material to construct other holes. It also takes skill and commitment of the golf course superintendent to make the water feature into a diverse, functioning ecosystem and not just a manicured, dyed water, sterile hole full of water.

NAPLES NATIONAL
GOLF CLUB

It's politically incorrect to categorize people, but if I had to name the three most notorious benevolent dictators of golf, I'd list Clifford Roberts of Augusta National, John Arthur Brown of Pine Valley and Dr. Charles Benton of Naples National. I never met Mr. Roberts, had met Brown only once, but could write a book about Dr. Benton. I am sure they were all three strong willed individuals who cared more about the golf course than most of the people around them, and as a result caused some long lasting hard feelings.

Charles Benton has a Ph.D. in biological sciences. Through some astute medically-related discoveries involving genetic engineering, he made enough money to retire young as a wealthy man. He loves the game of golf and became obsessed by the idea of creating a first-rate members club in Naples, Florida. So he searched out a 325-acre parcel of land and persevered through a painful permit process that required he put 150 acres into permanent wetland conservation, leaving 175 acres to work with. Then all he had to do was find a designer, secure funding, staff the place, sell memberships, and micro-manage the operation to perfection. He did all that, and did it well.

The par-3, 3rd hole can play as long as 193 yards or as short as 105 yards, from a tee complex that meanders through and around trees to the left. The rock walls of the tees blend together with the rock on the edge of the lake to unite into one continuous feature. Stately pines and puffy clouds provide a soft balance to the hardness of the rock.

Lying two to four feet thick above the coral rock strata is the sugar sand that most people associate with Florida soils. One goal we had at Naples National was to limit the maintained and irrigated turf areas to the smallest acreage possible and still have a playable, fun golf course. There are less than 50 acres of turf on the entire course, with the rest being sand scrub, such as here on the 560-yard par-5 4th hole.

Naples National was a hallmark project for us, our first course to make Golf Digest's list of America's 100 Greatest Golf Courses. This splendid course, kept in meticulous condition, has allowed us to compete and land other top quality projects whose developers might not have considered us before. Naples National is special, and so is Charles Benton and our working relationship with him.

Early morning on the 5th hole greets the first golfers with spotlights of color and textures. Behind the tee on this par 4 are ornamental grasses, a rock edged pathway and pink flowers. The tee is splashed in sunlight with mixes of shades and shadows into the native sand scrub area and fairway. The dew on the turf gives it a soft blue that seems to be a reflection of the sky.

Sand scrub areas, such as this one along the right side of the 7th hole, look like more of a hazard then they are. Actually, average golfers find it easy to play from this because they can ground their club and the ball sits up nicely. Scattered plantings of ornamental grasses or ground covers are really the only hazard, especially once they mature.

The 9th hole is a mid-distance par 4 that can play easy to a right front hole location, and dang tough to a left back one. Because the water level in the pond is tied to the ground water, which can fluctuate four feet or more up and down, the lake banks are designed and lined with coral rock to allow a clean edge during both wet and dry seasons.

I'm not sure why Dr. Benton even called me for an interview. Maybe it's because I also have a Ph.D. and, knowing how hard one must work to earn that degree, he figured I must have a work ethic that matched his. Anyway, I put together my best slide show and prepared an outline for an hour-long presentation on why we should be chosen as his golf course architect. About 10 minutes into the interview, Dr. Benton held up his hand and said, "Thank you, I've heard enough." I was stunned. I hadn't even gotten to my good stuff. I muttered something like, "Thank you for your attention and this opportunity," and hit the door. To say the least, I was dejected. I began to doubt if we'd ever really have a chance to land such a high profile project.

About two weeks later, Dr. Benton called me and said, "Well, we're ready to start." I had no idea what he meant. "Does this mean we have the job?" I asked. In typical Benton fashion, he answered with a question. "What do you think it means? How soon can you come down here?"

It is nearly impossible to look at a picture of Naples National without seeing stacked coral rock, rock excavated from the site about four feet down. Most other Florida golf courses bury the rock or treat it as fill. To make Naples National different, we left the rock exposed and used it in various ways. Here the coral rock lines the pond on the 12th hole, which transitions from native sand scrub onto golf course turf. This par 3 hole plays a maximum of 217 yards, but the carry over the pond is only 150 yards. Front tees have no water carry.

I was stunned again, but the next day I flew to Naples to meet with him and walk the property, as he had already done dozens of times.

At this meeting, I asked Charles what kind of golf course he envisioned. He answered that he wasn't going to tell me. Then I questioned what courses would he compare it to? He wouldn't tell me that, either. He didn't want us trying too hard to make it like some other course. He wanted his golf course to be different, to be "the most unique golf course in Florida".

Once again, I was stunned. There are over a thousand golf courses in Florida. Most of them are built on the exact same flat, swampy land with the exact same vegetation and soils and end up with the same necessary lakes and ponds. He wanted something unique, but wouldn't give me a clue as to what he envisioned. "Look," he said. "I hired you to give me answers, not questions." On the plane ride home, I made a list of every conceivable feature I'd ever seen on any golf course in the world, including every manmade architectural device. Then I started scratching off those that were common to Florida golf courses. After that, I scratched off outlandish and impossible ideas for this course, features like oceanfront holes and 60-foot high sand dunes.

Finally, I had narrowed the list down to stone walls. Dry-stacked stone walls are common in New England, where the walls were built to separate farms, and in Ireland, where they crowd the narrow winding roads. Many stacked rock walls were retained when courses were built in New England and Ireland, probably because they were too costly to remove. But south Florida had few rocky attributes, and no Florida golf course I could think of had any stone walls. What you do find in south Florida is coral rock beneath the three-or-four feet of topsoil. It's ancient coral rock, in layers four-to-eight feet thick. Usually, when golf course builders unearth coral during construction, they blast it loose, dig it out to create lakes, then get rid of it by dumping it in deep fills and covering it with sand. Sometimes, some of the coral gets used as bulkheading around lakes. But nobody used it to create stone walls on a Florida golf course.

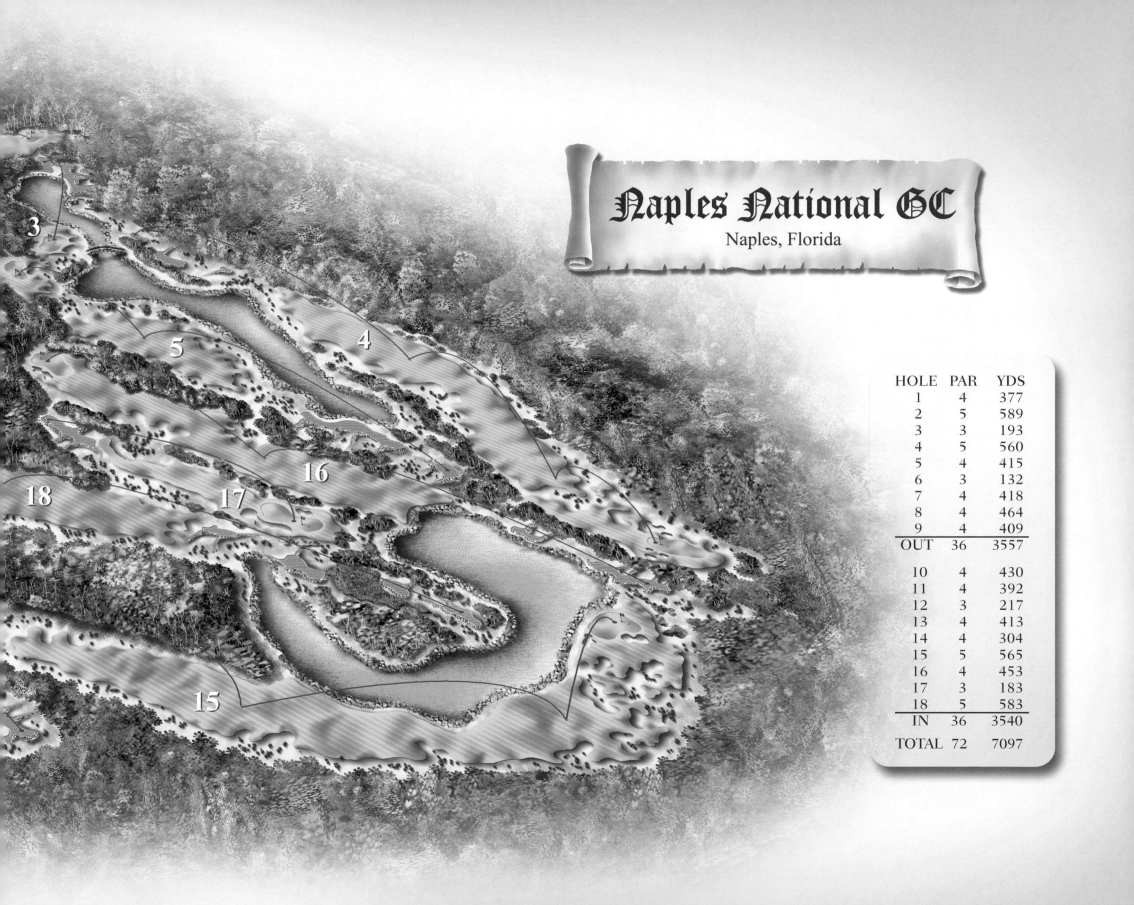

Naples National GC

Naples, Florida

HOLE	PAR	YDS
1	4	377
2	5	589
3	3	193
4	5	560
5	4	415
6	3	132
7	4	418
8	4	464
9	4	409
OUT	36	3557
10	4	430
11	4	392
12	3	217
13	4	413
14	4	304
15	5	565
16	4	453
17	3	183
18	5	583
IN	36	3540
TOTAL	72	7097

So on one of the routing plans we did for Dr. Benton, I added some stone walls to provide color, texture and height to the golf landscape. He liked it because it was indeed unique. When I questioned him where the walls should go, he said, "Just do what you think is right. If I don't like it, I'll take it out."

But once construction began on the golf course, the stone walls became an obsession to Dr. Benton. Not only did he lay most of them out by himself, he also laid out the locations for stone cairn tee signs. If workers didn't build walls that were perfectly straight, he'd make them tear them out and start over. Today, the stone walls are the signature of Naples National, and to me they're a symbol of a group of founders determined to make the best possible golf course they could.

Using coral rock to build support walls for tees such as on the 17th hole saved precious fill material from being wasted in outslopes, gives the tee an interesting look and is easy to maintain. The rock also adds a different textural and color quality than the green turf, brown pine straw and native sand scrub areas.

Dana and I could tell hundreds of stories about Dr. Benton, and for better or worse he is no longer part of the club. He was uncompromising in his demand for perfection from everyone who worked for him. He had phenomenal vision about what it would take to make a first-class club stand out among its peers. He coddled no member. Dr. Benton was a bit reclusive, gruff, headstrong, and to some, even a little abrasive. But from what I've read, so were Clifford Roberts and John Arthur Brown. The quality of the golf clubs they left as legacies attest to their passion.

The clubhouse at Naples National is distinct and striking. On the par-5 18th, it seems to be an extension of the natural sand scrub area because of its color. The rock edge along the lake that guards the front of the green acts as a subtle divider between golf and clubhouse area. Taken altogether, everything seems in scale and balance.

There are lots of fabulous golf holes at Naples National, holes wrapped around wetlands, cypress hammocks, and significant trees. Dana's bunkering emulates low, rolling sand dunes, and the green surrounds are tightly mown chipping areas similar to Pinehurst No. 2. That alone was enough to qualify it for Top 100 status. But the people who've been attracted to Naples National make it just as distinctive, guys like Fuzzy Zoeller, long-drive champion Evan "Big Cat" Williams, and many CEOs of multinational companies who love its low-key atmosphere.

Short and sweet is the 6th hole that stretches just to 130 yards or so, yet remains one of the hardest holes on the course. The green is small and turtle backed, with a little pot bunker and a large pine tree guarding the front. Perhaps it is the sand scrub pine straw and stone walls just off the tee that distracts the golfers' attention, or maybe because the hole looks so easy, but many seem to choke a bit here. Regardless, this is a signature hole that seems painted from natural materials on a flat site.

I was tickled to be asked by a previous client, my friends from the Country Club of Scranton, Pa., to design a wonderful new country club for them in nearby Moosic. But the first time I saw the property, I saw nothing but granite rock outcroppings, gigantic wetlands, steep hillsides and abandoned strip mines bisected by county roads in one direction, and a huge gas pipeline in the other. There wasn't a bit of topsoil on the site. My reaction was deflation, mixed with a little despair and a whole lot of doubt. But ultimately I became determined to make the proverbial silk purse of a golf course out of this sow's ear of a site.

At the time, I didn't really understand the character of the people who live in and around the infertile valleys between Wilkes-Barre and Scranton. These are tough people who've clawed out a living from this land for generations. Many became extremely wealthy and powerful business leaders. So where I saw problems, they saw opportunity. So what if we had to blast away tens of thousands of cubic yards of rock? Or re-establish a huge lake out of a coal mine sediment trap? Or tunnel under a county road? Or even find, haul and process hundreds of thousands of dollars worth of topsoil?

Color, texture and height are the artistic elements that golf course architects have to work with to make pretty pictures. Strip those elements away from this gorgeous 1st hole, and you simply have a nice 589-yard long par 5. With them, you have a memorable golf hole.

Some of the flat land we had to work with was made that way by previous strip mining for coal. Although it was flat, it was usually solid rock with no topsoil or, worse yet, covered in mine spoil, which is usually too acid to support plant growth. So on holes like the par-5 14th, we hauled away as much of the bad stuff as possible, drained the area and then capped it with a good soil. The left edge of the hole is defined by a protected stream.

I came to understand that the reason these folks could afford to build this course was because they didn't like to spend very much money, unless they were sure they had a winner. Without question, Glenmaura was the most physically difficult course construction job that any of us had worked on to that time. Bill Kubly of Landscapes Unlimited says it is still the most difficult that his company has ever handled. But we had the confidence of our friends, and they knew no fear.

Our associate Guy Quattrocchi was selected to live on the site as day-to-day design coordinator, and much of the success of the project is due to his ability to analyze a problem, find a solution, sell the idea to our bosses and then encourage the builders to go above and beyond the effort expected of them. Even today I marvel at what was accomplished at Glenmaura National, especially given the expenditure of time and money available to build it.

—

◄ *An autumn shot taken from the pro tee shows the trees we saved, as well as the protected wet meadow in front of the tee, the walk bridge over a mountain stream and the green beyond. The 7th hole plays from 193 yards to as short as 97 yards, depending on which tee you choose. As the distance gets shorter, so does the required carry over these natural areas.*

*We usually try not to introduce a par 3 hole
until the 3rd or 4th hole on each nine, but with an existing
pond and a great backdrop we decided to break our rule for this 11th
hole. From the pro tees, the hole plays 152 yards with nothing but water
and sand from tee to green. This is penal design in its purest form.
However from each set of tees to the left, the hole becomes less penal, with
the forward tees aimed directly down the fairway to an open green front.*

During the time Glenmaura was being built, Aureus was the big dog in the very competitive golf apparel industry, and a major employer in this part of Pennsylvania. One of their celebrity representatives was Larry Mize, who had won the Masters in 1987, chipping in to defeat Greg Norman in a playoff. Larry was retained as a design consultant in the later stages of construction, and he offered many good design ideas that help make the golf course so exciting. (He suggested the back tee on number eighteen that, even with today's high-powered golf equipment, requires an enormous drive to carry a couple hundred yards of bedrock scraped clean by a glacier 10,000 years ago.)

This is the 8th, or quarry hole as seen from the right rough short of the landing area. The green is set on the other side of this old strip mine area, so a long drive must be accurately placed to the left of the quarry to set up an easier approach on this 417-yard par 4. If the golfer loses the drive or approach shot to the right, it is probably a lost ball.

There are many spectacular holes at Glenmaura, in fact almost every one of the 18 could qualify as 'the signature hole' on most golf courses. Each has a special blend of off-site views, wide fairways framed by rock walls or sheer cliffs, bisecting streams, huge trees and splashy white sand bunkers. The 8th plays up to an old quarry on the drive, and then requires a daring second shot across the quarry to a right-rear hole location. The seventh has a large waterfall as the backdrop to a green set right against a creek.

Glenmaura National GC

Moosic, Pennsylvania

13

12

11

10

©2002 Donald A. Keller

HOLE	PAR	YDS	HOLE	PAR	YDS
1	5	589	10	5	542
2	3	205	11	3	152
3	4	463	12	4	413
4	4	405	13	4	387
5	4	430	14	5	581
6	5	516	15	3	240
7	3	193	16	4	412
8	4	417	17	4	384
9	3	196	18	4	385
OUT	35	3414	IN	36	3496
			TOTAL	71	6910

Glenmaura's 4th hole is a risk-and-reward par 4 that temps golfers to shorten the dogleg by driving the ball to the right of center and thus lessen a couple of clubs for the second shot. But miss the ball to the right, or cut it too close, and the reward can quickly become a rather severe penalty. Again, no matter how you play it, we want you to enjoy the scenery.

The PGA Development Tour, (now called the Nationwide Tour) has played an annual event at Glenmaura for the past few years and its players have voted it "the best conditioned on tour," as well as one of their favorite venues. Players in the Men's Division II NCAA played there and loved it too. Without question, Glenmaura National is a strong, demanding, beautiful mountain golf experience, but I think the real reason that people enjoy and remember it so well is because of its people. This is a special part of America and so are the good folks who live here.

It has been said that a great hole should look as good from the green as it does from the tee. This is certainly true of the 18th. The wide fairway is split by driving bunkers, and a long carry over the wetland to the left fairway allows more margin of error for the second shot to this stream fronted green.

≺ *Many of Glenmaura's golf holes, including this 413-yard par-4 12th were carved out of a mountainside. The 15-foot-high rock wall to the right of the driving area was created by drilling and blasting away thousands of tons of rock. When working in such terrain, the most difficult task is developing wide landing areas such as this one.*

From the 18th tee on a fall day, there is a sense of being part of a giant floral arrangement, as trees, wetlands and golf course plants display their fall colors. Larry Mize was the PGA tour pro consultant on this project, and from Larry's tee, only the strongest can carry the wetland short of the fairway on this 385-yard-long hole.

From its Pacific coastline to the Canadian Rockies, British Columbia is definitely God's Country. When we were invited to design a golf course just outside of Vancouver, above the town of Coquitlam, on an area known as Westwood Plateau, we were thrilled. The site was about 1,700 acres of steep granite mountainside, with several broad plateaus, salmon spawning streams, massive trees and teeming wildlife. The first time I walked the site, I felt like I was in the scene from the movie Return of the Jedi, where the skycycle race weaves through the forest. It was more than a little spooky, especially after I saw my first bear.

A portion of the site had been used as a road racing track, and since I still do a fair amount of road racing, I was especially intrigued. I was told stories about a hump in the track, just before a 180° turn, where faster cars and bikes went airborne. That very spot is now the 18th green, a tribute to the old track, its racers and the hairpin turn.

This is a good view of how placing tees diagonally around a hazard can make the hole fun and fair for all golfers. From the back tee, the 3rd is a 190-yard carry over a ravine, which is 100 feet deep at the right clearing line. Each tee forward requires less carry and the front tees line up to the green for no carry. Regardless of where and how you play this 3rd, you will always remember it.

The 1st hole on any golf course should play quickly but contain enough features so that golfers' sense of anticipation is aroused for the holes ahead. Here, the 1st hole plays across the corner of a scenic water hazard to a wide forgiving fairway defined by bunkers, then to a wide open green. To handle the 10 feet of annual rainfall the course receives, we installed lots of drainage that golfers will never see.

Canada's foremost golf course designer was Stanley Thompson, who used a bunker style of great flowing capes and bays. We copied that style on many bunkers such as the par-3 6th hole. In fact, all the sand along the left and back is just one massive bunker. The old tree stumps in the bunker are remnants of past logging operations from the turn of the 20th century.

This was a huge project on a huge site, and thank goodness we were able to work with an extremely experienced team of engineers and planners, or we would have struggled. The original assignment was an 18-hole golf course and range, but on the other side of a small mountain was perhaps 100 acres considered unusable, given the dozens of huge electric towers across it and its steep, rocky terrain. Our firm has always endorsed golf learning centers, so as part of our planning process we drafted a complete golf academy for this valueless area, one that included a large, multi-story covered range tee, a short game center, putting greens, three practice holes and a nine hole executive course, with a separate clubhouse and amenities.

≺ *Looking backwards from the 11th green to the tee, it is easy to see why Westwood Plateau is such a wonderful place to live. The scenery is without peer, the ocean and the mountains are only minutes away, and the climate supports lush plant growth, not to mention beautiful golf courses.*

When the price of developable land is extremely high, developers are willing to go to great lengths to save the couple acres of land that a par 3 hole requires. The 12th hole was literally blasted out of a granite mountain slope, in places 20 feet deep. But the result can be an awesome 162-yard hole like this. The tree trunks left in the stream corridor in front of the tee will be successive homes to insects, woodpeckers, then cavity nesting birds, and finally decay organisms when they topple into the creek.

Our main boss was an Iranian fellow who left his country when the Shah did, and took with him almost as much money. He didn't play golf. So when we explained our plans, we first presented the routing for the main championship course, and then as a sidelight we mentioned the learning center. He listened intently, then said he wanted the learning center built first, which surprised us. Normally, the main course gets built first to establish an identity. But our boss insisted he could sell more houses because of the learning center than the full-size course, and he proved to be right. The Westwood Plateau Golf Academy opened in 1994, over a year before its big brother, and quickly became wildly profitable. Within months, there were over 600 juniors in the lesson program, the place was packed from daylight to dusk with all manner of golfers and the restaurant was always crowded. This experience reaffirmed our conviction that golf learning centers are great for business and should be part of every golf complex.

Steep, rocky terrain is very difficult to build in unless the designer uses lots of sheer high walls such as the one behind the 13th green, or engineered stone walls such as the one on the right of the 13th fairway. The trees on the site were so dense and tall that some areas like along the left of this par-4 fairway rarely get sunlight. Golf course architects and superintendents need to identify those problem areas early and seek acceptable solutions, like using special shade-adapted grass types.

Westwood Plateau G and CC

Coquitlam, BC, Canada

HOLE	PAR	YDS	HOLE	PAR	YDS
1	4	352	10	4	382
2	4	347	11	4	342
3	3	205	12	3	162
4	5	535	13	4	350
5	4	470	14	5	523
6	3	196	15	4	456
7	5	583	16	3	180
8	4	415	17	5	501
9	4	341	18	4	430
OUT	36	3444	IN	36	3326
			TOTAL	72	6770

©2002 Donald F. Keller

HURDZAN · FRY
Great Golf by Design

The main Westwood Plateau course took over two years to construct. Every day seemed to expose more major challenges. Fortunately we had the foresight to have an onsite design representative there on a daily basis. We'd hired a bright young man named Warren Henderson, who previously worked for some guy named Nicklaus. Warren is brilliant and hard working. He later worked for Rick Smith and now works for Gary Player Designs. Warren and Dana were a dynamic duo and seemingly did the impossible, but not without a number of heated discussions with contractors, other consultants and even our boss.

Formerly this site was a road racecourse for cars and motorcycles, and this 18th hole was built right along one of the old straight ways. The area of native grass back to the right of the tee is where much of the ripped up pavement was buried. This had to be one of the most beautiful settings in the world for a racetrack, and now it is one of the most beautiful for a golf course.

Looking from behind the 17th green back uphill 501 yards to the tee, you can get some sense of how severe the slopes were. From the trees right and left of the fairway, you can imagine what the original side slope was and how much was cut along the cart path-side of the fairway. Although a little of that fill was used on the opposite side of the fairway, most of it was used to build the green pad and the ridgelines behind it. The big bunker protects the hole location shown here, from what are usually short third shots on this par 5.

The golf holes at Westwood Plateau are epic in their size and scope. The par-3 third hole plays over a 100-foot-deep chasm, the 12th hole was blasted out of the side of a mountain and the 15th drops 160 feet downhill, about as quickly as a ski slope. The 17th hole plays directly at snow covered Mt. Baker, and as I said, the 18th green is on the raceway hump.

The bunkers are a tribute to the splashy, flashy style of Stanley Thompson, Canada's greatest golf course architect.

The tee shot on the 15th hole drops about 160 feet to a ➤ fairway that was raised about 30 feet to the height of the retaining wall. A creek crosses well in front of the green, which is situated on a large flat area. The hole measures 456 yards long, but it plays much shorter, perhaps 60 yards shorter. This was one of the most difficult holes to permit and build because of its steepness.

I no longer find Westwood Plateau to be spooky, although there's still a sense of immersion into the wilderness when playing a round on the course. The tall, majestic Douglas firs, huge glacial boulders, deep ravines, and meandering streams provide isolation and serenity. The adjacent upscale housing is dwarfed by the panoramic views of snow-capped mountains to the north and the broad river valley to the south. Its total golf experience has earned Westwood Plateau a very high ranking in Canada's SCORE magazine as one of the "Best in the West."

This is one of Dana and my favorite pictures, and if you love golf and nature, you cannot help but say "Oh my God," when you walk onto the tee at the 347-yard, 2nd hole. When a designer has offsite views like this, his approach should be to design a nice place to play golf, and not try to make the golf features compete with the surroundings. Simple shapes and subtle grades are the way to go.

IRONHORSE

Dana was born and grew up in the Kansas City area, where he became a well-known and accomplished junior golfer. So when we were invited to submit a proposal to design a golf course in the upscale suburb of Leawood, Kansas, we put our best efforts into it, for there is nothing quite as fun as designing a golf course that your friends will play. We were thrilled to be selected and even more delighted to work on the project with two very competent engineers, Phil Gibbs and Brett Haugland of Continental Engineering. We were a team from the beginning and it was a pleasure blending our respective skills together and seeing our efforts produce a dramatic golf course.

Golf courses are not only appropriate and natural places for wildlife, they are also wonderful settings for art. This magnificent carving, sculpture and landscaping blend together three artistic pursuits into one incredible experience. This is the entry feature to a special place called Ironhorse.

If you study the creek bank separating the par 3 2nd's tees from the green, you will notice some rock ledges. The elevations of this hole were established to avoid that rock and any drilling or blasting it would require, then appropriate tee elevations were decided upon. The backdrop is the clubhouse, which is designed in the style of an old train station, appropriate for a golf course named Ironhorse.

The course was named Ironhorse for an abandoned railroad right-of-way that ran through the property. The land also has a nasty little winding creek, both dramatic and subtle contour changes, and is punctuated with great sycamore trees and limestone outcroppings. The golf course was to be the centerpiece of a housing development by the same name. The developer transferred land to the city of Leawood, in exchange for a promise to build an outstanding public golf course. From its initial opening, the golf course has won awards and was ranked the number one public course in the state for a long time.

Split fairways are often just architectural gimmicks because one fairway is always more preferred over the other. But on the 11th hole, the choice is more complicated and equal. Choose the lower fairway and you are left with a shorter approach shot if you avoided the creek along the end of the fairway and the right side. The upper fairway takes the creek out of play on the drive, but leaves a longer approach.

From this view of the 13th hole, you would never guess how densely populated the adjoining areas are. Golf courses are well-suited to preserve open space, trees and habitat areas that might be otherwise lost to development. This golf course has become home to deer, ducks, and all sorts of other critters, not to mention some neighborhood golfers.

As with all golf course developments, we started with a site-constraints map. A main roadway bisected the property. The creek and its flood plain established a reliable source of water, if worked within wetlands and streams regulations. There were some very hard surface rock layers, a high tension power line easement and the need to integrate housing. Fortunately, the developer gave us our choice of land but understandably requested we use as much of the creek flood plain as possible. Normally this isn't much of a problem, but this particular creek, although normally slow moving, meandered all over the valley and drains thousands of rooftops, streets and parking lots from upstream development. When it rained upstream, the property took on a pretty substantial amount of flood water. Building a golf course in a flood plain is a good use for land that otherwise would have little or no value, but it requires some design and construction techniques that are usually learned through experience. We had no problem dealing with the flood water, but fitting the landing areas between bends of the meandering creek was a big challenge. We also had our share of clawing holes into steep rocky hillsides, but the final product is a nice mix of experiences for golfers.

Although Ironhorse is in a built-up neighborhood, it is isolated from the houses by a wide creek that flows behind this par-3 green, and by trees that frame the other sides. The downhill shot from the back tee on the 12th is 190 yards, but it can play as short as 80 yards. The green is actually in a flood plain, which is a good use for such land.

HOLE	PAR	YDS	HOLE	PAR	YDS
1	4	405	10	5	555
2	3	211	11	4	371
3	4	425	12	3	190
4	5	518	13	4	387
5	3	212	14	5	481
6	4	405	15	4	372
7	4	340	16	4	380
8	4	408	17	3	199
9	5	555	18	4	475
OUT	36	3479	IN	36	3410
			TOTAL 72		6889

Ironhorse GC
Leawood, Kansas

9

3

2

8

4

7

6

5

©2002 Donald H. Keller

IF
HURDZAN·FRY
Great Golf by Design

Our favorite hole would surely be the 11th, where a natural rocky creek wanted to remain where we thought a fairway should be. So we compromised with Mother Nature, left the creek and put part of our fairway on each side of it. On the long par-4 18th, necessity required that we play atop a ridge created well above the level of the creek, but that could only be done by cutting through rock. We dug and ripped and scraped all the way from the creek to the green. By then, we had exhausted the contractor as well as the budget, so we stopped. The result is a high sheer rock wall along the right side of the green. It seems to be the perfect finishing touch for a golf course with such a strong sounding name as Ironhorse.

Some smart person once said, "Simplicity is the essence of good taste." That same description could apply to the 10th hole, a 555-yard long par 5. No mounds, no flashy white sand, no flowers - nothing but a creek, a wide landing area, a couple of bunkers and some trees. Taken together, this is a wonderfully simple hole.

Although a portion of the fairway is in the flood plain of the creek, most of the 9th hole is above it. The 9th has two routes to approach the green. The more direct route must carry the creek on the second shot, while the safe route is to lay up to the right of this view leaving a medium length approach. The tree to the left forces the decision of whether to play to the left or right.

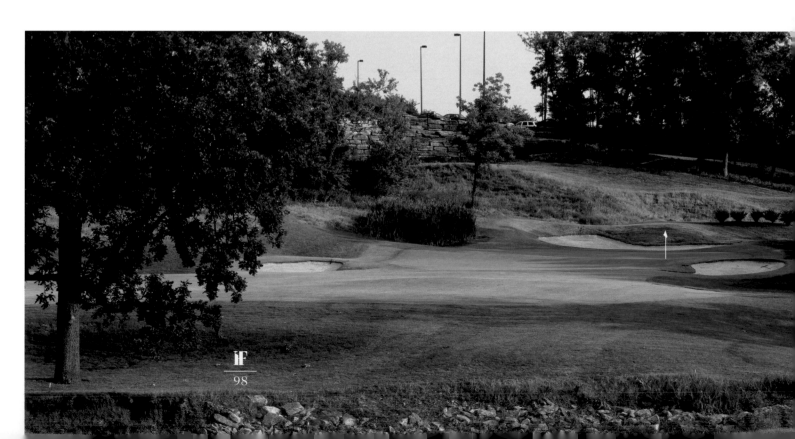

Getting irrigation water to the site was no small feat, for the creek had an unpredictable flow pattern, there was no chance of sinking a well in the rock that underlaid the course, and processed city water was not an option. But being the creative guys they are, Phil and Brett of Continental Engineering came up with a plan to take water from the Blue River and pipe it several miles to a storage pond on the golf course. It was a brilliant idea that has worked well and has given Ironhorse a dependable water supply. A couple of other neat features are the clubhouse designed in the style of an old-time train station, their logo of a horse, and the golfing learning center. The golf academy at Ironhorse preceded the First Tee program by many years, and is a perfect prototype that demonstrates Leawood's futuristic thinking. It includes a very large double-ended range to separate golf groups from daily golfers, a short game center to develop those important around-the-green skills, a large putting green and three practice holes on which to teach the rules, etiquette and procedures of golf. Many others have built similar facilities on spare ground, but in Ironhorse's case, Leawood officials bargained the developer out of a piece of very valuable and developable land. I believe that demonstrated a real commitment to grow the game, and is another reason why the city of Leawood is such a desirable place to live.

The par-3 17th has many elements that make it interesting. First is the wetland in front of the main tees, then the creek along the left side and very close to the green. The floodplain and back hillside trees nicely frame the green setting isolating it from development. This is a good example of how holes can naturally fit into an environment.

As I mentioned, Dana grew up playing golf in Kansas City. He hung around mostly at an old municipal course in Swope Park, a Tillinghast design, and made friends with the regular crowd. Over the years, he's established many standing bets with these guys, most of whom are decades older than he is and know all too well how to adjust at the turn. Nowadays, whenever Dana goes home to visit his parents, he tries to arrange a game with the old Swope Park gang at Ironhorse, a course he knows very well. They still find a way to take his money.

We try particularly hard to make the finishing hole as climactic as the end of a fireworks display, and some sites make that task easy. The par-4 18th hole is such a site. From the back tee, the tee shot is over the creek, while the other tees are situated to the right for easier angles. The second shot must carry a second creek to another wide approach area short of the elevated green surrounded on the back right by a natural rock wall that we shaped a little with blasting.

StoneWater sounds like a name that some big-bucks ad agency created. But truthfully, the name just evolved. Everywhere on this golf course site where we found water, we also found stone - lots and lots of stone. This was a bit of a surprise because soil-testing on the site generally showed four to six feet of soil overlying bedrock. But like so many things in golf course architecture - and life - you must be prepared for unexpected problems and come up with logical solutions. So the stone at StoneWater not only provided us with a course name, but also another course feature. Our golf course plan that originally had very few stone walls on it, now has thousands of feet of them.

Normally, rock is irregularly-shaped and of random sizes, while stone is more predictable and uniform. The stone at StoneWater naturally fractured in flat slabs about four inches thick and broke into rectangles a foot or two across. It was perfect for stacking and as there were thousands of cubic yards of it, we used it to line lake and stream banks, the sides of tee boxes, the fronts of some greens and wherever else the look of stone would add to the aesthetics of the golf course.

Island greens have become a little too common, and hence are almost unimaginative as well as unfair for many golfers. However, the peninsula green never seems to go out of style, and serves the purpose of challenging good players with left side hole locations, while being entertaining and fun for average players with middle and right pin sets. The 7th is only a 353-yard par 4, from even the pro tees.

StoneWater is located on the golf-rich east side of Cleveland, not far from The Country Club (William S. Flynn), Canterbury (Herbert Strong), Shaker Heights (Donald Ross), and Beechmont (Stanley Thompson). All those courses are on wonderful rolling land with babbling brooks, magnificent trees, and little or no adjacent housing. By comparison, the StoneWater site was flat and wet, with insignificant trees, more wetlands than we could babble about, and lots of adjacent housing. But unlike our predecessors, we had powerful earthmoving equipment, a fairly large construction budget, and the modern technology of improved grasses, automatic irrigation and sophisticated drainage to produce a course of superior design and maintenance.

Preserved wetlands not only serve vital environmental functions, they can also add some color and strategy to a hole like the par-5 4th. The fairway squeezes down between two small wetlands, challenging the big hitters on their drives and the average golfers on their second shots. From the black and white striped fairway marker it is 150 yards onto the green, which is fronted by a stone walled creek.

One of a golf course architect's greatest challenges is how to design a golf hole with a forced carry on the second shot that is fair and playable for weaker golfers. One method is to choose to cross the hazard at its narrowest spot, set the driving zone to end just short of that area, then measure backwards to locate tees at comfortable distances for each golfing segment. Such deliberate thought produced the par-4 9th hole of 470 yards.

Most of the StoneWater site was a wet woods of red and silver maples that grew tall and spindly because of competition for space and light. Building the golf course and managing the woods will allow the strongest among them to reach maturity and their full stature. The par-4 10th is a good example of that transition starting to take place. Because the site was so flat and featureless, we chose to use a dramatic bunker style to define and highlight play areas.

We also had a well-to-do industrialist for a client who made one of the club pros in the area his partner in the venture. It was a great team and the golf course wasn't denied anything we felt it needed. It was a story that ended sadly with our client selling his interest in the course to settle a domestic matter and the new owners replacing the golf pro. Despite those setbacks, the golf course remains as testament of an involved and spirited team of friends working towards a common, beautiful goal.

The view from behind the green of the 247-yard 17th gives a good idea of the relationship of groundwater to finished golf course grades. Fill from the pond was used to elevate the tees and green and allow the woods on either side to remain at natural grade.

StoneWater GC

Highland Heights, Ohio

2

3

4

9

8

7

5

6

HOLE	PAR	YDS	HOLE	PAR	YDS
1	4	432	10	4	364
2	4	464	11	3	193
3	3	201	12	4	417
4	5	559	13	5	626
5	4	362	14	4	338
6	3	173	15	4	433
7	4	353	16	4	423
8	4	390	17	3	247
9	4	470	18	5	557
OUT	35	3404	IN	36	3598
			TOTAL	71	7002

The golf course plays in a big figure 8 of a routing, so no holes are noticeably parallel and adjacent holes are separated by sufficient space and trees to give each hole a sense of isolation. We were able to do sufficient earthmoving to create the illusion of rolling ground, with many tee shots playing downhill to wide fairways. Water and stone comes into play on most of the holes, but in different ways. On some holes, they're a wide, shallow, flat bottom brook. On others, it's a deep, still, narrow stream, or a rock-edged lake, or a backwater, or a manmade wetland or detention basin. Overall, StoneWater is a study on how to blend water and stone as naturally and artistically as possible within the necessary artificiality of a fine golf course. Dana did an awesome job of crafting a golf course that stands proudly among some of the best works of the best designers to ever work in Ohio.

◁ *To affect overall site drainage, it was necessary to create small areas of open water and then add wetland areas to their edges. One such pond/wetland fronts the par-3 17th green. Since there was so much stone on the site, we used it to edge ponds and tees in places to give a crisp edge and add another color and texture to the landscape.*

The name StoneWater was used because everywhere we found one on this site, we found the other. By continuing to use stone and water together, edging the pond in front of the 18th back tees, and building the waterfalls and creek channel on the left, the golf course developed its own identity and signature. This par 5 of 557 yards is a strong finishing hole.

On a side note, when the original team of developers was going strong, they came across a larger- than-life-sized sculpture of an old Scotsman in early 1900s dress, with a bag of wooden shafted clubs, his hand raised to shield his eyes as he peered into the distance for his golf ball. That sculpture was the work of Brad Pearson, a golf course superintendent from Holdrege, Nebraska who does this kind of golf art during his long winters on the Great Plains. Brad's sculpture so captured the spirit, tradition and love of the game that the partners not only bought the piece to serve as a focal point to the clubhouse, but used it as their club logo. The logo persists today, and we were so impressed with Brad's work, that a copy of that beautiful work of art now serves as a focal point of the office of Hurdzan/Fry Design in Columbus, Ohio.

There is always a danger in design of overworking a good idea or theme, so finding the right balance becomes an artistic endeavor. On a flat, wet woods site, visual interest can be created by blending together colors, textures and elements of stone, water, sand, grass and trees. We believe we found a very eye pleasing balance of those elements on the 201-yard par 3, 3rd.

For many years, the city of Palm Desert, Calif., simply filled space between glitzy Palm Springs and the golf fanatical development of PGA West in LaQuinta. However, this low key community was quietly acquiring property, developing a well-balanced tax base, and planning an infrastructure that was as progressive as it was efficient. Palm Desert also had a deep-seated interest and respect for the environment, and sought to control development to preserve the assets of the desert that attracted its residents in the first place. The city set the example by using desert-adapted landscaping on its public lands to conserve water as well as establish an identity that is unlike the flowers-and-green-grass look of neighboring communities. The city was also acquiring a sizable development fund, and when the time was right, they decided to build a golf complex that would be environmentally correct.

When the requests for proposals for this project came out, we asked our good friend John Cook, then a Palm Desert resident, to be part of our team. We'd previously worked with John in designing the Cook family golf course, Cook's Creek, near Circleville, Ohio. We interviewed and were ultimately selected to do the 36-hole project. Other than a 45-hole golf course we'd designed in Japan, this 36 holes would be our biggest project ever, and our first on the west coast.

The great variety of plant material that can survive in the desert, if given drip irrigation, is quite amazing. When it is artistically integrated with the golf course in out-of-play areas, surrounded by decomposed granite fine gravel, and backdropped by stark mountains, the effect is intensified. When we started building the 176-yard par-3 14th, it was a flat and wind blown barren field. Now it is a golfing paradise of dramatic colors and textures.

But as things often happen in the competitive business of golf course design, a dark cloud blocked much of our sunshine when a hotel corporation, brought in to establish a resort hotel at the facility, declared us to be unknowns (except for John, of course), and insisted on a celebrity design firm. Even though we had a signed contract and were committed to the work, we were asked to relinquish our rights so another designer could be hired. We're all big boys in this business, and there have been other times when celebrity design firms have taken projects away from us. That's just part of life, although it normally happens before a contract is signed. Anyway, we reluctantly agreed. But then some members of the city council felt that the demand for a celebrity designer was unconscionable.

One major design objective in the desert is to keep structures low profile so as not to block views of the surrounding mountains. The 9th green on the right, 18th green on the left, and the clubhouse in-between are all low-profile.

They worked to convince the remaining council members that we were the right choice and that our contract should be honored. When the city of Palm Desert told the potential hotel developers it was Hurdzan/Fry or nobody, we were ecstatic. The deal with those potential developers ultimately fell through. The site was 600 acres of desert, drifting sand, scraggly bushes, junked cars, occasional foundations of squatters' homes and not much else. We were instructed to design two environmentally-correct golf courses, with no housing on one 18, but leaving room for a few hotel sites. The other 18 should allow for some vacation condos. Otherwise, we were free to move as much earth (or rather sand) as needed, build as many recirculating streams as we wanted, and add as much landscaping as was necessary to make this the crown jewel of public golf in the California desert.

This 3rd has the distinction of being the first golf hole pictured on the front cover of Smithsonian Magazine. The magazine did a feature on environmentally-correct golf courses and the water-saving approach of our Desert Willow courses was a prominent example. This par 3 is far easier to play than it looks from this back tee of 194 yards. Turfgrass was minimized and replaced by desert plants and decomposed granite. Today the plant material is mature.

It is amazing how quickly vegetation grows in the desert when given a little drip irrigation. This is another picture of the 3rd hole, taken just a few years after the one used for the Smithsonian magazine cover. Especially compare the vegetation that forms the backdrop to the green.

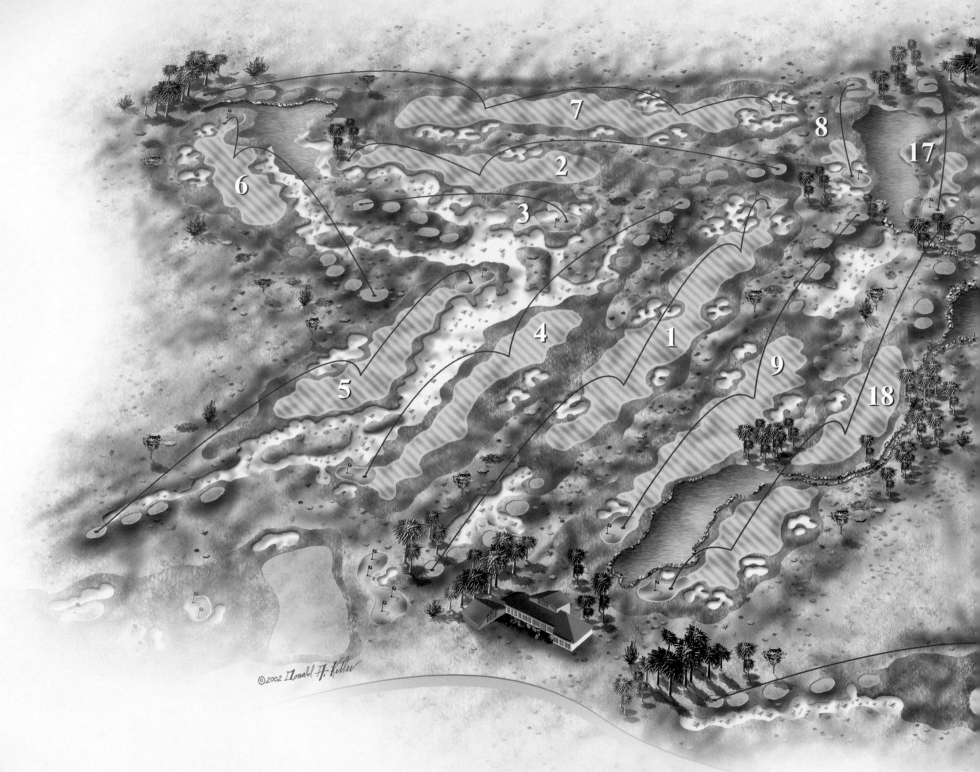

HURDZAN · FRY

Great Golf by Design

©2002 Donald H. Keller

Firecliff Course

Desert Willow Resort Palm Desert, CA

Desert Willow
Golf Resort

16

15

14

13

12

11

10

HOLE	PAR	YDS	HOLE	PAR	YDS
1	5	535	10	4	435
2	4	410	11	4	452
3	3	194	12	4	427
4	4	446	13	5	550
5	4	429	14	3	176
6	4	331	15	4	332
7	5	569	16	4	420
8	3	155	17	3	204
9	4	455	18	5	536
OUT	36	3524	IN	36	3532
			TOTAL 72		7056

Our friend and long time associate Guy Quattrocchi lived on the site and guided the day-to-day construction work. It began by wetting the sand for about 30 days through constant hard irrigation. Moist sand can be worked and shaped, but dry sand blows around and is too soft to support most construction equipment. Over a million cubic yards of material was moved on each course to create hill and valley landscapes of epic portions. We fit most golf holes into the valleys to protect golfers from the constant wind, to reduce evaporation of precious water from irrigated areas and to provide containment to errant golf shots.

Since there are two golf courses at Desert Willow, we tried to give each a different personality, which is difficult in the desert where choices of plant materials is so limited. After much discussion it was decided the first golf course, called Firecliff, should be capable of hosting a PGA Tour event. So we made it hard to score on from the back tees, provided lots of spectator viewing areas and a dramatic finishing sequence of holes. The second course, named Mountain View, is shorter in length, has easier shot values, far less bunkering and is integrated with some housing.

We purposely limited golf turfgrass to about 75 acres on each course, about half of that found on traditional golf courses. The remaining areas were covered in decomposed granite (known locally by the initials d.g. and often called "desert gold"), which formed the foundation for our desert landscape plants. We spent a fair amount of time studying natural oasis that occurs along the San Andres Fault, only a few miles away. Our objective was to reproduce the feel of that oasis wherever we had water features on the golf course. We also studied rock formations, desert plants and plantings, and what worked and didn't work on other golf courses. We were fortunate to work with a pair of veterans of desert landscape design, Eric Johnson and Chuck Shepardson, who helped select and properly place xerophytic plants.

IF

An old song lyric goes, "A desert is an ocean with its life underground," but with water the stark desert landscape can become a kaleidoscope of color and life above ground. The key is water, even if it is recycled effluent water, as is used on our Palm Desert golf courses. The rock faces are manufactured copies of existing rock formations found in natural oasis that occur along earthquake fault lines. We worked with landscape architects to blend oasis-type plant materials into the golf course, such as the par-3 17th on the Firecliff Course.

This unique approach earned the Firecliff course the cover picture of the April 1997 issue of Smithsonian Magazine (just months after it had been planted), and recognition for its environmental sensitivity. The course also drew accolades in Natural Geographic Explorer Magazine, a half-hour feature on the Discovery Channel, and numerous other awards.

To appreciate the real distinction between the courses, you must play them. But no matter your playing ability if you love the desert environment, enjoy the mountain surroundings, and appreciate the high level of attention to detail that Kemper Sports Management provides, Desert Willow should be on your "must play" list.

Sunrises and sunsets in the desert are special times of day, for long shadows accent each undulation and plant. This view is of the 8th green and the mini-oasis behind it, with desert scrub and the mountains as a backdrop. Note the color of the mountains now compared to mid-day. The hole measures only 155 yards from the back tee, so all golfers can relax and enjoy this view.

PALM DESERT, CALIFORNIA

The Mountain View course at the Desert Willow Resort was designed to be a transition between the more challenging and tournament quality Firecliff course, and the traditional Palm Desert course of fence to fence turfgrass, flowers and flowing water, and surrounded by housing. Mountain View was intended to have each of these characteristics, but with it's own distinct personality. This meant a grading plan similar to Firecliff of having the holes graded into valleys, creating elevated viewing areas and development pods, but with smaller and fewer bunkers, almost no forced carries and a little less distance. The result is a golf course that is less demanding than it's big brother, but is just as scenic and aesthetic.

The one feature that distinguishes the two golf courses, and is a good study in golf course architecture are the green complexes. Unlike Firecliff, Mountain View was purposely designed with more forgiving greens, target areas and hazards that make the course easier to play, without sacrificing the dramatic look of the tournament course. "Looks hard, plays easy" is a great description for our design intent. Specifically, Mountain View greens are more open in the front, right front hazards are easier to avoid or get out of, and the putting surfaces have fewer contours to confound putting. These are subtle differences that have profound impact on playability, and something that requires many years of designing to master. If you get a chance to play both courses, you will understand the difference that such small variations can make.

————————————

The variety in texture, heights and colors of desert adapted plants is quite striking to golfers, especially when seen integrated together as on the 5th hole. The key to making this an enjoyable golf experience is the blending of these visual impacts, with golf holes that have only a few traditional hazards like bunkers.

There is a special feeling about naturally occurring desert oasis that we have tried to recreate when using water as a design element. Specifically, we copied the width and tumble of the creeks or streams, the density and types of vegetation, and the relative size of pools or transition areas. Therefore, we are very pleased with how the par 5 6th hole turned out.

≺ *The Mountain View course was designed to <u>look</u> as challenging as the tournament quality Firecliff course, but play easier. Although the surrounding and framing desert vegetation is the same on both courses, notice how the 1st hole on Mountain View has landing areas which are wider, the grading and vegetation in the desert scope rough is lower and less dense, and the front of the green is very open. Bunkers on Mountain View are also fewer, smaller, and shallower.*

Soft and gentle grades distinguish ≻ most of the holes on Mountain View as shown by this photo of the 3rd hole. Steeper and higher grades are used to raise teeing areas and frame the holes, but the overall concept was of an "open" feel, so views of the distant mountains allow them to seem like part of the hole.

Another difference is that the Mountain View golf course is part of a resort property developed by the Intrawest Company. Intrawest is famous for its' development of villages at North American ski areas, that put the cars underground, the shops and businesses at ground level, and the living areas on above ground floors. By removing the cars, everyone walks everywhere, including the bars and restaurants, the shopping areas and even to the ski lifts. It is a friendly, slow pace of life feel that folks enjoy, and Intrawest wanted to bring to their golf condo properties. Naturally, the village concept would not work, but developing a unique sense of place would, especially if it was tied into other passive recreation such as walking or biking.

The golf features on the par 3 8th hole on Mountain View are really quite simple if you strip away the desert vegetation and the mountain backdrop. But with them, it produces an exciting hole with strong visual qualities. The point is that when a designer is given a great setting, the golf features should not or need not compete with it.

Golf courses in the desert transcend the simple oasis concept, but in fact, they have many similarities. Water is vital to both and pools of blue water are common to oasis, along with the density and type of scrub and tree vegetation that is pictured here. However, most important is that both golf courses and oasis provide man with a sense of security and serenity while being reminded of the hostile and inhospitable environment that surrounds them. The 18th hole at Mountain View is a good example.

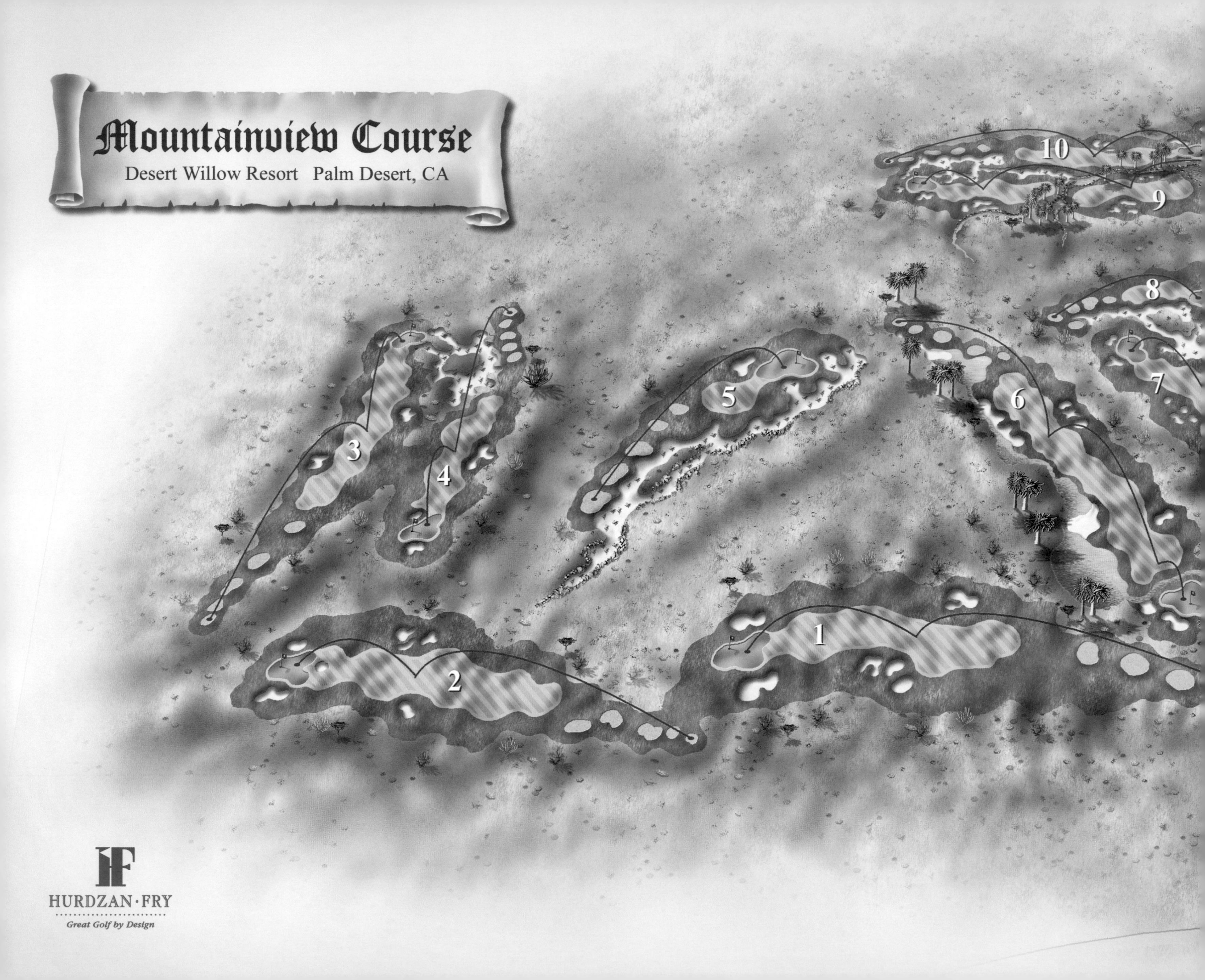
Mountainview Course
Desert Willow Resort Palm Desert, CA
1
2
3
4
5
6
7
8
9
10
HURDZAN·FRY
Great Golf by Design

HOLE	PAR	YDS	HOLE	PAR	YDS
1	4	419	10	4	410
2	4	390	11	3	200
3	4	453	12	5	501
4	4	374	13	3	199
5	3	227	14	4	448
6	5	476	15	4	426
7	4	390	16	4	386
8	3	179	17	4	342
9	5	555	18	5	533
OUT	36	3463	IN	36	3445
			TOTAL	72	6908

Desert Willow Golf Resort

©2002 Donald A. Keller

It was an exciting challenge working with the development planners and Palm Desert officials through the entire process because it was extremely complex. The golf course routing and grading plan was the backbone of the development plan, so all grades for the entire property had to work together, along with the roadway and circulation system, the overall site drainage plan, the utility infrastructure, walking and biking trails, the phasing schedule, along with establishing buffers to neighboring land uses. This was artistic engineering at its best, and who better in our firm to assign such a formidable task than Bill Kerman. Bill has just the right blend of engineering skills, golf course design, common sense, patience and stubbornness to handle any project, no matter how large or how complex, even one like Desert Willow. The naturalness of the finished product belies the enormous planning effort and construction coordination it takes to produce a course like Mountain View. It has won many architecture and engineering accolades, but most important to us, it is a fun, memorable place to enjoy golf, as well as enjoy the peace and quiet of desert life.

———————————

Golf in the Palm Desert area started to proliferate in the 1970's, and has never really slowed down. Much of the reason lies in the fact that golfers are drawn by a special brand of "summer" golf when the calendar says "winter". If it weren't for the stark mountain backdrop, this 17th hole would look like tens of thousands of other holes across America during the warm seasons. So Mountain View is a great name to remind us that this gold course is in a special place at a special time of year.

Most Palm Desert golf courses were developed to enhance building lots, and often those housing units are placed so close to the golf holes that they hide the true magic of the Coachella Valley. At Desert Willow we were encouraged to place the quality of the golf experience above the lot density and as you can see by this photo of the 9th hole what impact that has. This shows the antithesis of "condo alley" and why golfers are attracted to the openness of Desert Willow golf resort.

Part of our obligation to our clients is to design a golf course that will help them achieve their financial goals. We've never failed on that obligation, and sometimes we've been able to help them exceed those goals. Sand Barrens Golf Club is a case of exceeding expectations.

Edson and Malcolm Robertson are brothers who've run several businesses about 25 miles south of Atlantic City, New Jersey, the principal ones being a campground and RV sales. The Robertson's are young and determined, with a great respect and balance for business, family, friends, golf and other finer things in life. Edson is the tight-fisted business guy. Mal takes on the role of a big-hearted, always-smiling facilitator. Together, they get their money's worth out of everything they do.

When they decided to get into the golf course business, they had a clear vision of what they wanted when they hired us. We all were very deliberate in our planning and worked extra hard, but the main reason for the success of their Sand Barrens Golf Club is that the sandy soils of the site were so perfect that it could pass for a laboratory-selected and blended root zone for putting greens. And that sandy soil was hundreds of feet deep throughout the property. That meant it not only was a perfect growing medium for turfgrass, it also offered perfect drainage. It's not uncommon for two of the largest expenditures in golf course construction to be drainage and rootzone modifications. On this site, the Robertsons needed few of either, so they were saving hundreds of thousands of dollars.

———————————

A golf course architect's dream site is one of deep, sandy, well-drained soils that can be shaped and hollowed out without fear of creating drainage problems. All of the sand seen in this picture of the 1st hole, and in all other pictures of Sand Barrens, was sand naturally found on the site. Such sites allow for cost-effective construction and maintenance, long playing seasons and a golf course look that is difficult to achieve anywhere else at any cost.

Even though the Sand Barrens site was pure sand, there were places where ground water would stand and form wetlands if we cut down 10 to 12 feet. Creating such functioning wetlands was not required of the developers, but they agreed wetlands are valuable environmental resources, so they allowed us to build them. Draining excess surface water from the golf course into them also keeps these wetlands healthy through drought periods. This is a view of the 11th hole of the South Nine.

Grading bunkers down below existing grade gave them a unique appearance and allowed fairway grading that didn't visually block the bottom of trees. It gives the golf course an established and dramatic impact, such as on the 399-yard par-4 3rd on the South Nine.

From behind the 5th green on the West Nine, one can see how fairway, woods and wetland work together on this hole. This early morning photo with long shadows gives the hole a special feel.

What's more, almost the entire site was covered in scrub pine trees and bayberry bushes that effectively separate golf holes. It's easy to clear such undergrowth and replant it. The land is much like that of New Jersey's historic Pine Valley Golf Club, only the Sand Barrens site was nearly dead flat. The other positive aspect of the site was a good, clean, abundant irrigation source from wells.

Sand Barrens was always planned to be 27-holes, but when the process started Edson and Malcolm decided to only build 18 holes so they could see what things would cost, how good the course could be, and what kind of return on investment they might realize. They figured a third nine was years away. But once they saw the phenomenal response to the 18 from the day it opened, they decided to build the third nine immediately. The following year they built the clubhouse, which solidified Sand Barrens as one of the region's finest public golf courses.

The 5th hole on the West Nine is at the lowest part of the property and hence was the easiest place to construct wetlands. They run along the right side of most of the 514-yard par-5 hole, so a fairway was graded wide enough to make it easy to aim and play away from them. Besides the benefits of wetlands to the environment, they also add a great deal of interest to a golf hole.

What makes Sand Barrens so popular with daily-fee players? It's well situated, only an hour or so away from both Philadelphia and Wilmington, Delaware, and is very close to Atlantic City. The clubhouse is low-profile and large, but inviting. The staff places a great emphasis on friendly, helpful service. Once golfers catch a view of the lake and golf holes beyond the clubhouse, anticipation to get out onto the course grows. The course is not disappointing. It's a wonderful, relaxed journey off elevated tees to wide landing areas. Holes are framed by trees and menaced by ponds, deep bunkers and waste areas carved from the natural sandy soil.

At Sand Barrens, Dana had the freedom to build below the grade without worrying about drainage. He was able to define a hole with trees, then dig out deep bunkers and use the resulting soil to build gentle, graceful landforms. He was able to carve out some fairways, recessing them well below the tree lines. He turned huge pits into waste areas, giving their edges a special flair. He was able to merge fairways right into the greens, for the only difference is in height of cut. This allows for all sorts of interesting bounce-and-roll approach options. In one particularly creative moment, Dana designed a double green over 50,000 square feet in size. That's roughly as much putting surface as you'd find on an entire 9-hole course. At Sand Barrens, this green cost almost nothing to build. Dana simply shaped it from the existing soil.

≺ *The tee shot for the 6th on the South Nine, is downhill from a large fill area, then straight away to the green 546 yards away. The left-side bunkers tend to work into the fairway landing areas as they advance down the hole. The trees on the right accent this effect.*

Our grading concept was to build sandy scrub areas below natural grade and raise the fairways to get definition and strategy, and nowhere is that concept more apparent than on the 8th hole of the North Nine. The stairs in the sandy scrub show how deep the scrub area was cut, because the fairway is at natural grade. Since they are not bunkers, golfers can ground their clubs when playing out of them on this 595-yard par 5.

Sand Barrens GC

Swainton, New Jersey

HOLE	PAR	YDS
North Nine (White #)		
1	4	401
2	4	411
3	4	401
4	4	391
5	3	161
6	5	580
7	4	442
8	5	595
9	3	201
OUT	**36**	**3583**
South Nine (Blue #)		
1	4	365
2	3	188
3	4	399
4	4	439
5	4	439
6	5	546
7	3	204
8	4	295
9	5	511
OUT	**36**	**3386**
West Nine (Red #)		
1	4	386
2	5	561
3	3	175
4	4	398
5	5	514
6	3	203
7	4	384
8	4	448
9	4	440
OUT	**36**	**3509**
TOTAL N-S		**6969**
TOTAL N-W		**7092**
TOTAL S-W		**6895**

©2002 Donald H. Kolker

We decided to make only two or three fill areas on the entire course, and so they became huge and high - so big, in fact, they don't look like they were built. Each supports a tee complex for a couple of holes, presenting downhill tee shots on otherwise flat land, such as from the 9th tee on the South Nine, a short par 5 playing through a gauntlet of bunkers.

Dana practiced a gentle earthwork approach except for two major fills over 30 feet in the air that now serve as multiple tees. These fills are so massive they almost seem natural. After all, why would someone deliberately pile up dirt so high they could look down into a bird's nest? But Sand Barrens big hills work and golfers enjoy the view as well as launching shots from those elevated tees.

The bunkers at Sand Barrens are patterned after those at Pine Valley, and give the entire golf course a sense of movement and topography it doesn't really have. There are also a few sod wall bunkers, the most notorious being at the ninth green on the South Nine. Dana stacked the sod in that bunker himself, and he's one of the few who can get the ball out of it on a consistent basis.

Some holes like the 9th on the West are a mixture of bunkers and sand scrub areas. Often it is hard to tell the difference, but if the sand is raked, it is a bunker and golfers can't ground their clubs. Sandy scrub areas are usually larger and easier to play out of.

The par-3 9th on the North Nine plays across the irrigation storage pond and finishes in front of the clubhouse. The pond vegetation was actually designed and built into the pond to provide habitat value and naturalness. The water comes into play mostly from the back tees of 201 yards, while forward tees play over dry land.

There's no question that any sort of golf course on this site would have worked and made the Robertsons some money. But our compatible and cooperative effort at Sand Barrens resulted in more. It's been a huge financial success for them.

Occasionally, a golf course architect may find that a certain hole, can play to either of two green sites. Deciding which would make a better hole is often so difficult that owners suggest building them both and alternating play. So the par-4 4th on the South Nine can play to the left of a grove of trees to a lower green or to the right to a higher one. Another New Jersey course called Pine Valley has this same feature, on consecutive par 4s.

PEORIA, ILLINOIS

The vaudeville saying of "if it plays well in Peoria, it will play well anywhere," was supposedly based upon the observation that folks in Peoria, Illinois are hard to please. But after meeting so many nice people during our time working on WeaverRidge, I think the root of the saying lies in that Peorians (if that is a term), are honest in their opinion and they don't like wasting time and money on worthless things. We didn't know that when we started, however, we were aware of the vaudeville label.

Two prominent business people hired us, Dianne Cullinan who ran a large real estate firm, and Jerry Weaver who with his wife Nancy, were in so many successful and diverse ventures that they were hard to characterize. Dianne enjoyed golf while Jerry tolerated it, but they both agreed to be partners in a golf course and housing development on 370 acres of ground that the Weaver's owned. The land was a mix of rolling, fertile, crop fields, interspersed with woods and wetlands, and a wide but dramatic creek valley that was over eighty feet deep, and populated with all types of trees on the steep hillsides. It was not the typical flat farm land that we saw as we drove from Chicago to the site. In fact we had no idea just how pretty Peoria and the area around it really is, compared to what we imagined. But the varying elements that made the Weaver property so dramatic were also the main challenges we faced in routing a golf course. To make enough ground available for housing so that the deal made economic sense meant trying to find ways of putting the golf course on the least desirable ground for development, which was the steep hillsides, the creek flood plain, near wetlands and through the woods.

From the 18th tee, the fairway below looks hard to miss because it is so wide. But smart players can shave a few yards off this 556-yard dogleg-left par-5 by cutting the inside corner. Cut too much and a tree might snag your drive or the creek comes into play. The longest drivers can fly the creek and have a good chance of getting home in two.

Bill Kerman of our office did the routing we used as a doodle on a U.S. Geologic Survey map on the airplane ride home after his first visit. This proved to be the only one of a couple dozen we subsequently tried that actually worked. After finally conceding Bill's routing was best and the land planner was satisfied with lot densities, we completed our plans and specifications and bid the project out to a certified golf course builder.

Irrigation lakes and short par 4 holes like the 5th create an exciting chemistry of golf shots. From the back tees (387 yards), golfers can choose how much of the water hazard they wish to risk, to gain the reward of a shorter approach. There is plenty of room to bail out to the right, and shorter tees are placed to minimize the forced carry.

Although land seems stable, there are many dynamic forces working to change it, and none more so than flowing water. What seems a docile stream during dry times becomes a raging, eroding torrent during wet periods. To protect stream banks as well as help reduce maintenance of the stream channel, rock riprap is sometimes a requirement. This 489 yard par-5 11th hole crosses a riprapped creek twice.

Most people think of the Midwest as flat farm fields and for the most part they are right. But where creeks and rivers have formed valleys since the last ice age, the topography can be dramatic, steep and inhospitable for golf. So our design approach was to leave the trees along hillsides, like on the 10th hole, and utilize the creek as a front hazard for the green. Rock riprap on the creek bank helps define the edge of the hazard for the second shot.

The 11th was built from what used to be farmed cornfields bisected by a creek which we were allowed to move so we could build the hole as you see it. There is a false notion that agriculture is environmentally good for land, but somehow golf courses are not. Nothing can be further from the truth. If one uses the measure of soil protection, stability and diversity of wildlife and protection of surface and ground water from chemicals and fertilizer, golf courses are very healthy environments.

As construction began Dana made most of the weekly construction observation meetings, and since Jerry Weaver didn't know much about golf he was on site nearly every day. Dana and Jerry quickly became good friends and together solved all of the unforeseen problems of constructing the golf course. Jerry knew the farm well and had lots of great ideas that enhanced golf holes, like moving the third green closer to a giant oak tree, or adding a creek and waterfall system to hole number seven, or building the super high tees on the 12th hole. Dana would not only implement these changes but he would also stay at Jerry and Nancy's house on his visits, and soon Dana's whole family was spending a day or two with the Weaver's on Dana's driving trips back to his old hometown of Kansas City. I know for a fact that Dana enjoyed the experience, and I can only hope the Weaver's did.

The scale of the natural elements found in a green setting determine the scale of the green and bunker complex. It does not just happen on plans or in the field during construction without subtle adjustments to grades and faces. This 13th green shows Dana's ability to get it right in the field. This 441-yard long hole has excellent visual balance.

WeaverRidge GC
Peoria, Illinois

10

18

9

8

1

7

6

WeaverRidge

©2002 Donald H. Keller

HOLE	PAR	YDS	HOLE	PAR	YDS
1	5	540	10	4	418
2	4	391	11	5	489
3	5	519	12	3	228
4	3	182	13	4	432
5	4	387	14	4	406
6	4	388	15	4	458
7	4	435	16	4	439
8	3	194	17	3	187
9	4	381	18	5	556
OUT	36	3417	IN	36	3613
			TOTAL	72	7030

IF

HURDZAN·FRY

Great Golf by Design

Playing from one hillside across a constructed water feature to a hillside green makes for a nice par 3, like the 187-yard 17th. But building it so it is fair and fun for all skill levels of golfers is often a difficult task. Unfortunately this view only shows the finished product and not the days and days of earthmoving machinery it took to build it. (The outhouse in the background was an opening day joke from Dana and me to owner/developer Jerry Weaver.)

A big part of designing a golf hole is trying to provide good air movement to allow the grass to survive hot, humid summer weather. One technique is to open areas under trees by removing bushes and low limbs, as well as drainage corridors on surrounding hillsides if possible. The 14th hole shows this well.

Obviously the Weaver in WeaverRidge came from Jerry's last name, and the Ridge came from Jerry's insistence of building the clubhouse as far out on the ridge as possible to give views down the creek valley. As usual, Jerry made good judgments and the clubhouse is attractive, functional, and offers spectacular views. The golf course just missed winning Golf Digest's 1998 "best new upscale course" by 0.04 points behind Pete Dye's Bulle Rock.

WeaverRidge offers such a fabulous overall golf experience that it is not uncommon to see cars in the parking lot from all over the Midwest, especially from around the Chicago area. The golf course superintendent, Geoff Kemp and his wife have been there since early in construction to help prevent or solve problems, and now offers one of the best-manicured public golf courses in North America.

There is some old saying about "saving the best ➤ *for last," and that would apply to the 18th hole at WeaverRidge. The hole starts from tees elevated 80 feet above the landing area. Then the par 5 plays across a creek to a second landing area defined by trees and bunkers, and finally to a green at the base of the hill below the clubhouse. This was one of the first holes laid out on the routing plan because it was so natural and strong.*

So if you visit there and you are welcomed to the course by a middle-aged man with a big smile on his face and a kind word for everyone, chances are you just met Jerry Weaver. Jerry and Nancy spend a good deal of time at the golf course personally attending to all details be it as simple as picking up paper in the parking lot or waiting tables, for that is their style. WeaverRidge is a hometown, family run golf course that has a big city, resort feel. And by the way, it does play well in Peoria.

The 9th is one of our favorite holes because we did little more then draw it and build bunkers. A major creek flows in the trees to the left. What is now fairway used to be a hayfield. All along the slope to the right grow huge oak trees that make the 381-yard long hole feel as if it has been there for a long time.

ST. ALBANS, MISSOURI

The Country Club of St. Albans is part of a development that consists of 5,400 acres of wooded hillsides and meadows near the Missouri River, 30 miles west of St. Louis. It contains the evidence of some 200-year-old Lewis and Clark campsites, and encircles the small town of St. Albans, which housed railroad workers a century ago, but today has only a few homes. In 1990, Tony Novelly, an aggressive and intelligent developer, wanted to preserve what existed, but add a country club and upscale housing. It was ideal, a quiet country lifestyle in a historic setting with easy access to the big city.

The first course, named Lewis & Clark, was designed by Jay Morrish and Tom Weiskopf and opened in November 1992. We were selected to design the second 18-hole course, named Tavern Creek after the largest of four creeks that run through the site. The general topography of the land is broad, flat valleys set between very steep high hills, with a creek in every valley. As you may suspect, when it rains hard, these docile little streams get angry and often flood. When we first walked the land, we found the remains of several homesteads, hard-luck farms and family cemeteries. On our golf course alone, we had to route around several small burial grounds.

Wetlands, woods and native grasses contrast beautifully with the golf course turfgrasses on the 568-yard 11th. These areas are also good habitat for all sorts of critters that have traditionally lived on this site. The fairway is wide, the bunkers flat, and the rough is forgiving, so this par 5 plays much easier than it looks.

Tony has done well in the oil business, and then the Copper Mountain resort in Colorado. When Tony started St. Albans, he brought along an experienced team of planners and project coordinators who'd worked together before. These guys and gals knew their stuff, and they knew Tony, a big strong man who doesn't just walk into a room, he bursts into it, commanding your full attention. He is fearless when it comes to development, and will tackle and succeed at objectives that more timid developers would avoid. Tony knew what he wanted and where he wanted it. Our job was to figure out how to get it there, at a reasonable cost but a very high quality.

Tavern Creek, for which the course is named, flows along the left side of the 15th and then cuts in front and right of the green. The fairway bunkers are mostly to contain errant shots from reaching the creek, but they also help defend the inside of the dogleg on the 329-yard hole. As seen so often on this course, there are many unmaintained areas that frame the hole.

The green site for the 10th hole makes for an intimidating approach shot because it is uphill, on a small turtle back ridge. Bunkers narrow the opening to the green. However the hole is a medium-length 182-yard par 3, so such a green setting is appropriate and attractive.

Tavern Creek does not have returning nines. It plays out and back through the four large valleys and over some very high hills. The results are some very dramatic golf holes that derive personal characteristics from whatever dominant natural feature was found on that hole. On the second and fifth, it's one of the creeks. The 11th plays up a dramatic hill, while the 14th plunges straight downhill. The 10th features one of the small cemeteries while the 12th showcases a remodeled studio home. Tavern Creek itself prominently plays a key role on the closing three holes.

In order to make the golf course fit onto some of the ground, a considerable amount of earthmoving was required, which gave Dana a free hand to work his wizardry at producing dramatic settings. Dana is a genius at directing cuts and fills that seem to have neither a starting nor stopping point and simply flow from element to element, tying everything together.

The grove of pine trees is a bit unusual for this area, so the decision was made to save them and also make them part of the strategy of the 13th hole. By playing close to the pines, an accurate drive can significantly shorten the second shot as compared to a safer play line to the left on this 441-yard par 4.

The Missouri hills make a great backdrop to the golf course built in the valleys between them. The 16th hole has some wonderful movement to it simply because of contour planting and mowing. Much of the varied vegetation can come into play on this 474-yard par 4.

The 7th green backs up to Tavern Creek but it does not come into play unless a really aggressive approach shot rolls over the par 4 green. Instead, the green and bunkers were graded into the hilltop with soft shapes and low profiles on this 411-yard hole.

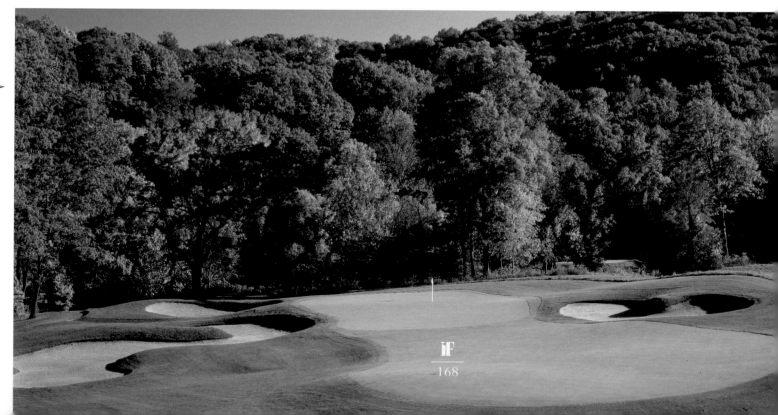

The par-3 14th had a natural brook running down the right side of the green site, so it made sense to dam up the water at the bottom, stone line the creek and recirculate the water. Not only is it aesthetic, the creek can come into play with right rear hole locations and from the pro distance of 236 yards.

HOLE	PAR	YDS	HOLE	PAR	YDS
1	4	409	10	3	182
2	3	177	11	5	568
3	5	510	12	4	387
4	4	385	13	4	441
5	3	162	14	3	236
6	4	449	15	4	329
7	4	411	16	4	474
8	5	529	17	3	224
9	4	398	18	5	524
OUT	36	3430	IN	35	3365
			TOTAL	71	6795

Tavern Creek Course

CC of St. Albans
St. Albans, MO

To construct the 398-yard 9th required grading a raised right edge of the fairway to buffer a wetland from golf course surface water, then reshape the steep left hillside to hide the cart path, and finally fit in a green between a pond and a steep hillside. Dana is a master at solving such grading problems.

If there's a downside to Tavern Creek, it's that its widespread routing demands the use of a golf cart. But that hasn't made it less worthy of its high ranking among the best courses in the state. It will only get better, for St. Albans is a quality-oriented development that continually re-evaluates itself, then raises its personal standards.

To the left of the par-5 8th, the creek is clearly visible, so it is easy to see how we use bunkers to act as containment features for shots that might be hit left. When a designer is fortunate enough to get a great site feature like Tavern Creek, the grading concept is low profile so as not to visually compete with it.

On the 18th hole, Tavern Creek crosses the fairway about 300 yards from the back tee, goes down the left side of the hole a couple of hundred yards more, and then turns right to cross in front of the green. Eighteen is a par 5 hole of 524 yards that perfectly fits the meanders of the creek. It is difficult to get home in two.

The view from the back tee on the 12th shows not only the downhill play line for this 387-yard hole, but also what has attracted people to the area for centuries. In the upper left you can see the Missouri River and just to the right of that is a high bluff that supposedly has a cave used by Lewis and Clark. The little town of St. Albans, which served as a train stop since the 1800s, is at the edge of the golf course.

I don't know why the early settlers to the Laurentian Mountains of Quebec named the beautiful river that flows through it Le Diable (The Devil). But the name stuck, and when Intrawest, the resort company that runs the world-famous Mont Tremblant ski area wanted to add another golf course along the river, the name Le Diable seemed natural for the course.

We were thrilled to be selected to design the course, even though the site has lots of steep, rocky slopes with not much topsoil. Spring comes late at this latitude and winter returns early, which is probably why this has been rated the best ski resort in eastern North America. But the site had many hidden blessings, not the least of which was a mountain meadow of pure sandy soil that we could truck in as topsoil.

Our first task was to create a routing plan that would, by necessity, move play up and down a small mountain on one nine, play the other nine in the fairly flat meadow on the far side of a major road, and make it feel like one continuous experience. The next task was to develop construction documents that dovetailed with the plans of the predominantly French-speaking engineers, consultants and environmentalists involved with a project of this magnitude, keeping in mind our French "weren't too good." Thank goodness they all spoke reasonably good English (although with a distinctively Inspector Clouseau accent), and we had Robbie Hellstrom as our point of contact. Robbie is bilingual, a powerful motivator of people, has boundless energy and had previously supervised the building of an earlier golf course at Mont Tremblant. He was the primary reason we were able to build the entire golf course complex in the space of six months. Until we saw it happen, we thought it was physically impossible.

Almost every golfer who has played here believes the par-5 5th is one of the best on the course, and yet it didn't take much to build it. The sandy soil reduced the need for drainage, the rock layers were shallow, thus obviating any extensive earthwork, but the natural contours allowed for wide play areas. This is a gentle uphill hole of 597 yards punctuated by outcroppings of rock.

Most mountain sites are usually devoid of topsoil. Probably because of glacial action, more than half of this site had deep layers of sand, which was clean enough to be used for waste bunkers, a very unusual feature on mountain courses. The 396-yard long 11th hole shows such a waste bunker. Also notice the steep face to the left of the green. The golf committee named this hole Fry's Wall in honor of Dana's devilish design.

Waste bunkers with MacKenzie-type shapes and undulations give the mid-length par-4 10th hole an unusual look. This bunker complex continues along the 11th hole, seen in the background.

Dana, Jason Straka and Robbie started in snowshoes in April, tying ribbons on trees for clearing. The clearing began in four feet of snow in early April. By September 1st, the entire golf course was seeded. Even today, all of us at Hurdzan/Fry think of Robbie as a miracle worker, as well as a friend.

The design concept was to fit the back nine into a rocky hillside, blasting away problem areas and disposing of the rock in an environmentally correct way, then plate the entire nine with sand taken from the front nine meadow. It sounded logical and simple, but doing it required some inventive engineering of haul roads and some incredible construction equipment. Intrawest, with its "No Fear/Can Do" attitude and extensive resources, provided both, and the golf course plan became a reality.

In mountains, there are times when building holes requires rock blasting. To minimize this expensive operation, it is best to limit such work to par 3s, such as the 12th hole. Here, only the green site and a small portion of fairway had to be drilled, blasted and hauled away, but it made for a dramatic green setting, especially from the pro tee 213 yards away.

Because the highway separating the nines is also the main entrance to the resort village of Mont Tremblant, it was decided to create two cart path tunnels under the road and no more. This sounds logical, but it wasn't easy, if we were to maximize the assets and narrow corridors we had for golf holes. But we worked it out and in the process created some superb golf holes, like the par-3 sixth hole that plays downhill 120 feet from tee to green. We're also fond of the 535-yard par-5 15th, which also plays downhill about 200 feet. But it was only a driver and short iron for John Daly when he played in a Canadian Skins game against Fred Couples, David Duval and Mike Weir.

_____

The elevation difference from tee to green on the ➤ par-3, 16th hole is only about 30 feet, but it appears to be much more because all the land around the green falls off sharply, especially behind the green. Just a 156-yard hole, the hole is still a bit intimidating.

One design objective in mountains is to place as many longer holes as possible on the flattest land. Even then, they may have strong cross slopes. The 435-yard 17th is a good example of how to utilize such a slope in a way that looks natural.

The 18th hole was built on a sandy meadow, which allows us to cut bunkers down into the site instead of raising them up, as is normally done on mountain sites. The result is a 561-yard hole that looks like it's in the Carolinas, not Canada. Notice the depth of bunkers left of the green.

LeDiable GC

Station Mont-Tremblant, Quebec, Canada

HOLE	PAR	YDS
1	4	459
2	5	550
3	3	199
4	4	389
5	5	597
6	3	221
7	4	479
8	3	202
9	4	411
OUT	35	3507
10	4	448
11	4	396
12	3	213
13	4	402
14	4	403
15	5	535
16	3	156
17	4	435
18	5	561
IN	36	3549
TOTAL	71	7056

11

12

14

13

©2002 Donald H. Keller

Dramatic mountain backdrops dwarf golf course features and flattens elevation changes. On the par-3 6th hole the drop from tee to green is about 120 feet over 221 yards, but it does not look it.

As the front nine meadow became the borrow pit for the topsoil of the mountain holes, Dana's approach was to create Pine Valley-type waste areas and bunker complexes for the meadow holes. That also saved a number of trees and provided a believable appearance to the grading and shaping. The finished meadow holes are unlike any other in eastern Canada and have become the signature of the golf course. Ironically, the native sand used in the waste areas, had a distinct reddish tint, which turned out to be perfect for a golf course named for the devil.

Fog rising from the Le Diable River provides an eerie backdrop to the par-3 3rd. From the back tee, it is a 199-yard carry across the irrigation pond, while each of the other tees is offset to the right to make the hole more playable for average golfers.

The par-5 15th hole is mountain golf at its best. It is all downhill, about 200 feet from tee to green, to a wide landing area, framed by trees and sheer rock walls. Beyond are a natural mountain lake and a small ski resort. This may be the prettiest, if shortest, 535 yards in golf.

The PGA Tour plays very few tournaments at municipally-owned golf courses, and just one event in a small upstate New York village. But since 1971, En-Joie Golf Course in Endicott has been home to the B.C. Open. Originally called the Broome County Open (for the county it resides in), it later became associated with the cartoon character B.C. The caveman and his friends were created by a local resident, Johnny Hart, who cares so much about his community he has allowed them to use his cartoon likenesses to symbolize and support the tournament.

The pro golfers loved the laid-back, old-time feel and hospitality of the B.C. Open, and for many it carried special meaning as the first tour event to which they were given a sponsor's exemption to enter. It's fair to say most tour golfers loved the tournament despite the small purse and somewhat funky golf course, a layout over which the adjacent Susquehenna River would flood a couple of times a year, depositing silt, logs and debris across fairways and greens.

A view of the 5th hole from where a well-placed drive would land on this 565-yard par 5, although touring pros blow it over the bunker on their drives. What makes this hole so interesting is that the next two bunkers down the fairway are 35 yards in front of the green, which forces all golfers to either lay up, play to the left of them, or try to carry them and roll the ball up the open green approach.

Although one of the longest standing PGA Tour stops, it is also an affordable city-owned public golf course, so it had to be easy to maintain with only a modest budget. This meant simple shapes, low profiles and wide-open play areas like on the par-5 3rd hole. Don't be fooled by its simplicity. At 554 yards, it is a good test of golf for even tour pros.

≺ *Trees are a large part of upstate New York golf courses in that they frame the land, and they frame the par-4 433-yard 6th. No attempt was made to make the golf features anything but low profile, for the trees would dwarf them as on this 6th hole. The trees are plenty of hazard.*

The moving force behind the tournament is longtime Endicott resident Alex Alexander. Alex got a grant to improve the course and hired Hurdzan/Fry to do the work. Our associate Jason Straka and I were happy to handle the remodeling of the course. I lived in Binghamton for a short while as a child and still had lots of relatives there. Jason had graduated from nearby Cornell University. Alex became a close friend who made us feel very comfortable, and far more important than we really are.

A major problem was that the work could not begin until after the tournament ended in late September, and had to be complete before winter, which sometimes came as early as November 1. So we had to remodel an old course, on small acreage with established tree lines, do it in two phases of about four weeks each over two separate seasons, and do it on a limited budget. We quickly saw it as a major challenge. Especially when flood levels can get high enough to almost cover the shelter houses on the course.

The first thing Jason and I did was map the flood water and try to find a way to raise the greens and tees out of the flood way, and then try to contain the rest of the flood to unimportant non-play areas. We were quite proud of our engineering, for the course has been flooded on several occasions since completion of the job without serious results after our improvements.

The 4th hole is a middle distance par 3 whose green was designed to have some very select hole locations that reward only the best of shot making. The source of strategy is the undulation designed into the green, with a general right-to-left slope and a valley that separates front to back pin sets. By far, the toughest ones are back left from the pro tees at 175 yards.

The par-4 15th was previously rated one of the toughest on tour because of its sheer length. When we remodeled the hole, it was shortened by 40 yards to 432 yards, with the green built right on a newly expanded lake. The closer one drives to the water, the easier the second shot. The contours in the green make most other angles very difficult.

The grove of pine trees is a bit unusual for this area, so the decision was made to save them and also make them part of the strategy of the 13th hole. By playing close to the pines, an accurate drive can significantly shorten the second shot as compared to a safer play line to the right on this 442-yard par 4.

I must admit our feelings were hurt after the first phase of improvements when some tour players were openly critical of our work during the following B.C. Open. I talked with many of them on Sunday after their round. That cooled things down, once they understood the plan. After the second phase of improvements, many of these same guys actually apologized and said they were learning to like the course. I think a big part of the grumbling was because the pros knew the old course so well. All they had to do before the remodeling was execute shots without taking into account much strategy. To score low on the new course requires lots of forethought about risk and reward. The same guys who gush about the 17th hole at TPC at Sawgrass complained about the new 16th at En-Joie. It's now a 321-yard par-4, where it's possible to drive the green and have a putt at an eagle, or lay up and go for a birdie. This devilish little hole has been pivotal in determining the B.C. winner several times.

15

7 5

8

6

16

17

En-Joie GC

Endicott, New York

HOLE	PAR	YDS	HOLE	PAR	YDS
1	4	367	10	4	356
2	4	379	11	4	441
3	5	554	12	5	545
4	3	175	13	4	442
5	5	565	14	3	212
6	4	433	15	4	432
7	3	188	16	4	321
8	5	553	17	3	185
9	4	407	18	4	419
OUT	37	3621	IN	35	3353
			TOTAL 72		6974

Before remodeling the par-5 12th hole, it was reachable in two by almost all tour pros. So to make it a bit more difficult, we moved the green back about 15 yards onto a hillside which raised it about four feet higher. Then a front bunker was placed to guard about one-third of the front opening, and a couple of rear bunkers make a low run up second a smart strategy on this hole of 545 yards.

There is an ethereal quality to every golf course, especially when long shadows cause a mix of light and shade across a golf hole. The area surrounding the golf course is equally serene giving the whole experience a restful quiet. This is the 8th, a 553-yard par 5 hole.

Because the flood plain is so flat, a series of ponds was necessary to allow for proper draining of the golf course. Placement of these ponds also made them part of the strategy, as at the 1st hole. It's just a short-to-middle iron approach shot on this 367-yard hole, but when the pin is located on the left side of the green, it is a tough par 4.

While we'd like to please everybody, we can't, so we don't worry too much about it. For every one armchair critic, there are dozens of regular golfers who think the new En-Joie is a great public golf course. Not only can you play where the pros play, you can do it at a very modest green fee. We are proud to be associated with the Village of Endicott, the En-Joie course, the B.C. tournament and especially Alex.

Perhaps the easiest hole to play and yet the most controversial is the 16th hole, a 321-yard par 4. It can be played by hitting two 7-irons or a long iron and a wedge, or a super-straight driver and a putter. It seems so many choices upset folks, especially when they choose the wrong way to play it. This hole has been pivotal in several B.C. Opens.

JERICHO NATIONAL
Golf Club

The four most common reasons to build a golf course are: 1) to sell green fees; 2) to sell memberships; 3) to sell housing lots; and 4) to sell overnight lodging. But every once in a while an individual comes along who wants to build a golf course for none of those reasons. He's not even a golfer, knows little about the game, but feels he should own a golf course. That describes a man we admire very much, Nick Karabots. A self-made millionaire in the printing and publishing business, Nick enjoys his success by renovating and restoring classic old buildings, a hobby that usually makes him even more money. Nick was one of the toughest, most business-savvy clients we've ever had. As a result, we've learned a lot from him and his family members in his businesses. Nick loves quality things but refuses to overpay for anything. Since he'd never built a golf course before, we had the tough job of convincing him to part with some money - a lot of his money, it turned out - to produce the quality golf club that is today Jericho National.

The name of the golf course comes from a nearby geographical feature called Jericho Mountain, which sits near the Delaware River in Bucks County, Pennsylvania, near the site where General George Washington and his troops crossed into New Jersey.

Nick not only bought a beautiful farm of several hundred acres and it's elegant manor house with indoor swimming pool, but he also bought several homes in the historic little river town of Brownsburg adjacent to the farm, where he is now restoring many of its oldest buildings.

On the far left hilltop, one can see Bowman's Tower, an area reportedly used by General George Washington's lookouts to keep track of British troops on the far side of the Delaware River, off to the right. They could also have watched golf played at the par-4 6th hole, had this golf course been there. Note the flowing tee edges, the wonderful collage of colors and the wide, friendly fairway.

As you look at this photograph of the 1st hole, try to imagine it as a wide sloping cornfield. That is what we started with. All a designer needs is modern earthmoving equipment, an owner who wants an extra special golf course, and an artist's eye like Dana's, to create this sweeping dogleg left par 5 that is a robust 577 yards from the back tees.

Often it only takes one feature to distinguish a great hole from a good one. In the case of the par- 3, 12th, that feature is the small necklace bunker at the base of the plateau green. The hole is a short iron or wedge for most golfers, but it is still quite intimidating.

To the uninitiated, it might have seemed that the farm was well-suited to a golf course and would require very little earthmoving to construct. Even I thought that until we started doing some routings and found that the naturally-occurring ridges and valleys occurred mostly in the wrong places. We were constrained by wetlands and a protected tributary to the Delaware River, as well as out parcels, county roads, state roads and a small development to the east. I shouldn't forget to mention this is Bucks County, affluent enough to not want or need any new development. So the choices we presented Nick were either a modestly priced but marginally good golf course, or a much more expensive but super golf course. As I said, it took a bit of convincing to get Nick to spend dollars, until he realized the quality the extra expenses would bring. The team convinced Nick he should go for quality, and quality he got.

This was a huge earthmoving project, because we had to cut hills and fill valleys to provide the proper sightlines, wide landing areas, positive surface drainage and space between holes. Rock layers further complicated the problem of earthmoving, as did the effort to save every tree possible, because Nick likes trees.

Jericho National has an impressive variety of golf holes. One of our favorites is the par-3 12th, just 150 yards from the back tee, with the green fronted by a significant bunker that is a mere 15-feet-deep but looks much deeper and more maniacal. Another favorite is the par-4 eighth that lies along the length of our irrigation pond. It looks much more severe than it really plays.

It is not often that there is a nice offsite backdrop to a hole that is certain to remain untouched. At the 13th, the pasture and barn will remain because the area has been declared part of a floodplain. This par-4 green setting is superb, accented by the very tall sycamore trees surrounded by a bunker. The tee shot is downhill on this 424-yard hole.

Jericho National GC

New Hope, Pennsylvania

4

8

6

7

9

©2002 Donald H. Keller

HURDZAN·FRY

Great Golf by Design

HOLE	PAR	YDS	HOLE	PAR	YDS
1	5	577	10	4	438
2	3	231	11	4	362
3	4	363	12	3	145
4	4	406	13	4	424
5	3	192	14	5	643
6	4	403	15	3	254
7	5	525	16	4	441
8	4	300	17	5	549
9	4	439	18	4	435
OUT	36	3436	IN	36	3691
			TOTAL 72		7127

Rolling terrain and cross-bunkers establish the strategy on the 525-yard par-5 7th. Low- profile grading and variation in bunker shapes keep the hole interesting to look at and enjoyable to play.

As an expert in buildings, Nick treated the clubhouse as his baby. His attention to detail can be seen everywhere, but for most golfers after an exhilarating round at Jericho National, the choice spot is on the large second-story balcony that provides breathtaking panoramas of the course and the colorful hills that make Bucks County so famous.

From the right rough, behind some cross-bunkers, this view of the monster 643-yard 14th shows how we like to use trees. They must be cleared wide enough to allow for good air and light penetration.

The irrigation pond on the left serves as a vital environmental adjunct to the woods and meadow adjacent to the golf course. This now plentiful supply of water will allow natural populations of plants and animals to flourish. The elaborate MacKenzie style bunkers help focus the golfers attention on the par 4 8th green, which is a drivable 300 yards from the tee.

ELLWOOD CITY, PENNSYLVANIA

Olde Stonewall Golf Club

Of all the nutty and wonderful people that we've worked for, Rick Hvizdak might be the king of unforgettable characters. Rick is a self-made wealthy man who appreciates his situation. His offhand business deals are legendary. Once he gets an idea, he seems to conjure up a special magic that turns it into a gold mine.

Who else would envision building an 18-hole golf course into the side of a mountain in remote Ellwood City, Pennsylvania and build a replica of an English castle for the clubhouse? Rick did.

Or put a restaurant in that clubhouse with food so good that it would draw people from Youngstown and Cleveland and the wait for a table would be at least and hour and a half? Only Rick.

Who would go to Europe just to buy medieval decorations for the clubhouse? Buy a rock quarry just to get enough stone for retaining walls? Buy a house, just to tear it down to add a few more yards to a back tee? Rick did all that.

Who would have the gumption to charge more than double the prevailing public green fee, compared even to Pittsburgh 45 miles away? Or turn down an offer of over $13 million for the course, clubhouse and restaurant. That's Rick Hvizdak, and that's Olde Stonewall Golf Club.

It is not hard to see where the name Olde Stonewall comes from when you see the 217-yard par-3 15th hole. So much stone was required that the golf course owner, Rick Hvizdak, went out and bought a quarry.

This view of the par-4 11th shows how steep the terrain is, and how beautiful the hillsides become when fall arrives. No one landscapes better than Mother Nature.

Even if Rick wasn't a financially sound risk-taker, he'd still rank as our most unforgettable character simply because he's a great guy to be with. Dana and I love to tell audacious stories about Rick, like the time a past president of the USGA was at Olde Stonewall and drove his golf cart too close to a tee. Rick went over and chewed him out with some pretty salty language. Rick is truly larger than life. Did I mention he made the maintenance building to look like a castle? Or that he bought a bunch of animal sculptures and placed them all over the course? Dana jokes that Chris Haney from Devil's Pulpit and Rick Hvizdak are running one-two in his favorite cult figure status, with Rick closing in fast.

The western area of Pennsylvania is extremely hilly and not an easy place to build a golf course. When working in such terrain, the designer must be willing to make huge earthmoving cuts and fills to create wide landing areas or else holes will be unplayable for most golfers. The 12th hole of 436 yards shows how to do it right.

A portion of the golf course is in the flood plain of the Connoquenessing River, and like most rivers in mountainous areas, they can become raging torrents in a short time. To reduce erosion of the riverbanks and possible damage to the golf course, riprap is used to line the bank, and it adds a nice look.

River valleys, mountains, autumn and early morning fog are a natural part of the change of seasons in Pennsylvania. Few golfers ever get to see the course when it is draped in heavy air and takes on a spiritual quality. Even regular players at Olde Stonewall may not recognize this as the 4th green.

Don't you get the feeling you don't want to hit your tee shot to the right on this par-4 13th? Bunkers can serve many purposes. Most of the bunkers on the right are to contain errant golf shots, not necessarily to punish them. The only real strategic bunker is the one at the right front of the green. Note the fairway contours that direct surface water.

Olde Stonewall is simply spectacular. Our associate David Whelchel deftly routed the golf course through some very golf unfriendly terrain, and Dana took on the task of making the golf holes work. Some holes flow gently across an old strip mine, others climb aggressively up the mountainside, still others seem to free-fall from bluff tops to perfectly maintained landing areas and one, the 474-yard par-4 16th, plays over two unmaintained protected-animal corridors to a hillside green. The hole is a thrilling adventure from beginning to end. In fact, so is the whole course.

The best testimony to the enjoyable brand of golf that Olde Stonewall offers is that golfers will willingly pay well over $100 to play it, and they play it often, even members of country clubs in the region. Olde Stonewall has even put Ellwood City on the map. Recently, a developer of a road racing circuit used the success of Olde Stonewall to convince investors and bankers that patrons would indeed seek out extraordinary experiences in their community.

The atmosphere at Olde Stonewall is fun loving, the golf course is challenging, the views breathtaking, and each round should be memorable. Just don't drive your golf cart too close to a green when Rick is there.

———————————

Par 3 holes like the 14th permit the designer to use tight ➤ *areas too small for other holes. There is a creek on the right, visible only as rock pools, and a super steep slope behind the green. The only way to use this land is as we did, with a 202-yard hole.*

HOLE	PAR	YDS	HOLE	PAR	YDS
1	5	569	10	4	463
2	4	392	11	4	436
3	4	399	12	4	436
4	4	434	13	4	400
5	3	174	14	3	202
6	4	436	15	3	217
7	3	150	16	4	474
8	4	425	17	4	371
9	5	502	18	4	464
OUT	36	3481	IN	34	3463
			TOTAL 70		6944

HURDZAN · FRY

Great Golf by Design

Olde Stonewall GC

Ellwood City, Pennsylvania

©2002 Donald A. Keller

≺ From this elevated 16th tee, it seems like a "grip-it and rip-it" drive to the fairway 150 feet below. However, the right side bunkers are definitely in play, and if a tee shot goes too far left, it is over a stone wall and into purgatory. Perhaps the best strategy is "smooth and easy" on the tee ball and try to make the best number your can on this 474-yard par 4.

↑ Depending on how you drove the ball on the 16th hole, your second shot might look like this. Once over the deep wetland ravine immediately in front of the bunker, the approach to the green is wide open. This hole plays much easier than it looks from the tee.

The 5th is a simple par 3 of 174 yards that demonstrates many artistic elements that make it special. The bunkers are large enough to establish and define shot values, but small enough so they don't visually compete with the wall, water and trees. Notice how the wall rises and falls and is accented by its own reflection in the water.

Trees, wetlands, an irrigation pond, bunker and wind all bother your drive on the 434-yard 4th hole Actually, they are the same things you need to consider on the second shot on this par 4, but taken together they make a pretty picture. The par 3 5th hole green is in the background.

Perhaps no other golf feature is as varied in size, shape, depth, placement, color or presentation as bunkers. Some styles just seem to work better on one golf course than on another. The style shown on the 399-yard 3rd hole is a blend of flat sand on the fairway ones and mild flash at the green. Regardless of style, bunkers need to read well, and these do.

One of the great pleasures in my life is in building golf courses. It's like that for most golf course architects and builders. That's why we're in a business that's so demanding of families. That's why we cope with crazy travel schedules, constant deadlines and the year-to-year insecurity, not knowing if there'll be work after the present job is done.

Glenn Rehbein shares that pleasure. He started a landscaping business with a used sod cutter and a beat-up pickup truck, and turned it into a huge, diversified family business. His first taste of seeing a golf course morph from dirt piles into mystical ribbons of green grass was as a subcontractor on a golf course built in northern Minnesota. That led to other projects and finally to qualifying him to do all phases of the work as a legitimate golf course builder. But golf course builders don't get much opportunity to be creative, as they're working with someone else's ideas. In the heart of most builders' festers a belief that, "Things will be different when I build my own course."

In 1998, Glenn decided that he was ready to build, own and operate his very own golf course, Troy Burne. The Rehbein businesses are located in the Twin Cities area of Minnesota, where everyone takes pride in the success story of native son Tom Lehman. Tom is not only a great professional golfer, he's a superb family man, a complete gentlemen, a thoughtful spokesman and a spiritual thinker. It was natural for Glenn to invite Lehman to be his design consultant on his dream course. We at Hurdzan/Fry were ecstatic to be selected by Glenn as co-designers with Tom, for we knew that these were all quality people who would produce a quality project on what proved to be a quality site. The actual site was just over the St. Croix River in Hudson, Wisconsin, only minutes from the Twin Cities.

The 2nd hole was a flat valley that had been farmed for crops and had no existing natural features. By developing the pond, we generated fill material to separate this 450-yard par 4 from the 5th hole to the right and enhanced the view from estate lots located further left.

As a contractor, Glenn knew that the better the drainage offered by the existing soils, the easier it is to build and maintain a great course. So he looked for glacially deposited landforms, one with lots of character and great drainage. The farm that would become Troy Burne had both characteristics, plus some spectacular views of the river hundreds of feet below. The site he selected would also serve a housing development, with a separate company developing the housing.

As we drafted the various routing options for Glenn and his housing development partner, we pushed the idea of a core golf course as much as possible by giving the bluffs and river views to the housing. The idea was to satisfy the requirement for high-priced lots without weaving the golf course through condo alleys. In addition to the sandy soils, the site was also blessed with two wide valleys, a fair amount of topographic change and some scattered patches of nicely-sized trees. These site features permitted us to route the course in the valleys, place housing on the high ground, use the topography to create varied shot values and use the trees to separate and isolate views and golf holes. Since Glenn and his company were going to build the course, we had a free hand to move large volumes of earth if necessary.

When a parcel of ground such as a cornfield has no natural features to distinguish it, the golf course designer has to produce interest through earthwork, colors and textures. The 18th hole is a good example of what Dana can create from nothing. This view is from the right rough in the driving area of the 470-yard par 4.

When we started construction there was no creek, no pond, no wetlands and no plateau for the 176-yard par-3 green of the 11th hole. All we had was a stand of skinny trees to separate this hole from the 14th beyond, and that was about it. The stream is lined and recirculated by a pump system, and it impacts five golf holes.

Looking from the 12th fairway across the irrigation pond and stream system to the 14th green gives some idea of the rough terrain and trees we had to work with. These pine trees behind the green separate it from the 11th green beyond.

Tom Lehman enjoys European links-style golf, and his 1996 British Open victory is a testament that he knows how to read the often-quirky playing conditions and develop tactics to deal with them. Tom made many, many great contributions to the design strategy of Troy Burne, but perhaps none greater than his insistence on having a flowing creek, or as they say in Europe, "a burne," to add a special flavor. Recirculating creeks are no big deal on most golf course sites, but when the soils are extremely sandy and the topography is significantly hilly, it takes an enormous amount of skill and expense to make it work. Because Tom was so emphatic about it, Glenn simply took it as another challenge to tackle. In the end, the recirculating stream became the namesake of the course, Troy Burne.

The 16th hole was set in a large valley that yielded another large pond, which was our borrow site to create the earthwork on the hole. The sandy waste area to the left may at first seem unusual until you realize that much of the site was pure sand deposited by a glacier 10,000 years ago.

Troy Burne GC
Hudson, Wisconsin

15

11

16

10

17

18

1

9

7

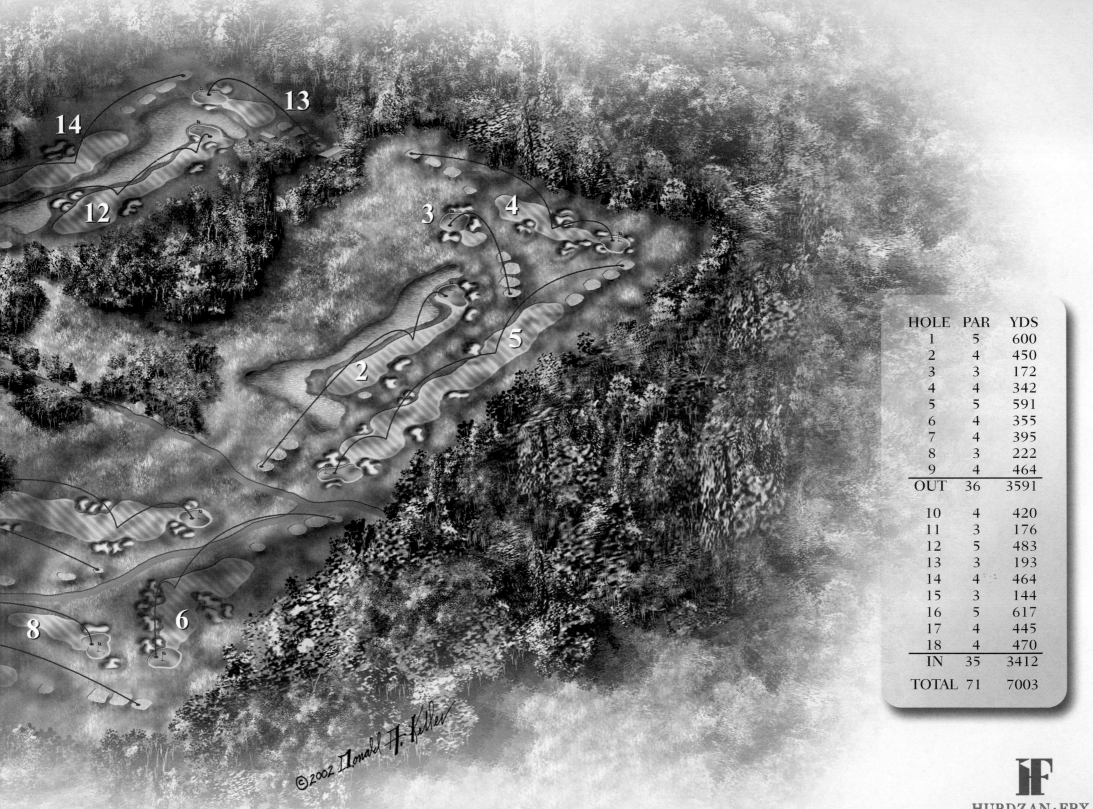

HOLE	PAR	YDS
1	5	600
2	4	450
3	3	172
4	4	342
5	5	591
6	4	355
7	4	395
8	3	222
9	4	464
OUT	36	3591
10	4	420
11	3	176
12	5	483
13	3	193
14	4	464
15	3	144
16	5	617
17	4	445
18	4	470
IN	35	3412
TOTAL	71	7003

©2002 Donald F. Keller

HURDZAN·FRY
Great Golf by Design

Another dramatic feature is the 10-foot-deep sod wall bunker in front of the par-3 15th green. This is another linksland trademark that seems to be at home in the side of a Wisconsin sand hill. In fact, there are dozens of features on this wonderful golf course that evolved through the lively give-and-take among Tom, Dana and Glenn. Take, for example, the 12th hole. It was the only location we could find for the irrigation pond, and Tom suggested

The valley gets smallest at the 17th green where a pond was created to control site drainage and yield fill material. The hole is 445 yards long, and from the elevated tee golfers can lay up in front short of the pond or place a drive next to it. This is a challenging approach shot from every spot on the fairway.

that his Troy Burne terminate in it. Dana and Tom settled on tee locations, Dana added the fairway contours and bunkers, and Tom designed the green. The reclaimed farm building on the hole, which serves as the irrigation pump house, restroom and rain shelter, was purely Glenn's creation. Together, this assembly of parts seems in perfect visual balance and has produced some exciting golf shots.

The few trees on the left were existing and kept, while everything else was created through earthmoving and shaping. Shaping with a bulldozer is both art and skill, which is why great shapers are highly paid. Since Dana shaped on many Tom Fazio golf courses before becoming a designer, he knows how to maximize a shaper's talent as shown on the 5th hole.

As with so many of our clients, Glenn, his wife Myrna and several of their sons who worked on the project, have become personal friends. We appreciate the trust and confidence that the Rehbeins showed in us, and we openly welcomed their ideas and concerns as we tried to fulfill one of life's grand dreams - building your own golf course.

———————————

There are many nice short par 3 holes like the 15th, but few have a sod wall bunker some 10 feet deep in front of the green. In front of the bunker is a protected wetland and habitat area, but there is plenty of bailout to the right. This green is massive which makes the 144-yard hole seem shorter than it really is, so the front bunker gets lots of visitors.

From behind the par-4 10th green, the pond that separates the 10th from the 16th hole is daunting. More importantly, it makes the view from the clubhouse spectacular. Note the waste bunker that runs along the lake and becomes part of the hazard strategy of the 16th hole.

This is another view of the created stream system and irrigation pond that separates holes 12, 13, and 14. The little barn between the 12th green and 13th tee is really the pump house that also serves as a rain shelter and restroom. This building was Glen Rehbein's idea, and a good one it was.

Dundarave, admittedly an unusual name for a golf complex, is an old Scottish family name. To those who've not been fortunate enough to visit this golf course on Prince Edward Island of the Atlantic provinces of Canada, the island has become synonymous with leisure. Being the smallest province, and an island to boot, PEI is best known by tourists seeking the mythical home of Ann of Green Gables, the best tasting mussels in the world, and a relaxed pace of life. As the island is now connected to New Brunswick by the 13-kilometer-long Confederation Bridge, PEI is becoming the golf destination of eastern Canada. One of its main golfing tourist attractions includes Crowbush Cove, Golf Digest's Best New Canadian Course in 1994, and the different but equally dramatic Dundarave course of Hurdzan/Fry.

Like most small island communities, everyone knows everyone else, and their politics. The life history of Dundarave begins with a series of legal and political maneuvers that seemed to be documented in the Charlottetown newspaper everyday, with each side alleging some kind of self-serving motivation by the other side. We read all of it, didn't understand any of it, so we just enjoyed the wonderful world of PEI while we fashioned an 18-hole golf course, a 9-hole executive course and a huge learning center. Dana, Jason Straka and I worked on this project, and when time got short and we needed more supervisors we called in Guy Quattrocchi.

From the tees on the 8th, your eye is first drawn to the end of the peninsula where you see the green on this 387-yard long hole. Once you gauge how much headwind you must allow for, then you must determine how much of the dogleg and bunkers you want to risk. Daring play can cut tens of yards off the second shot, or it can result in disaster.

To avoid stirring up old politics, we will limit the cast of characters to Robbie Hellstrom - who many thought should have been named "Hell Storm" for his well calculated and precision guided fits of anger. Robbie again did what we thought was impossible -- complete a golf course complex on PEI in less than five and one-half months. Even today, we are in awe of Robbie's ability to get things done, even if it means some people end up seriously disliking him. Robbie showed us what he could do at Mt. Tremblant when he was the project coordinator for the Le Diable course, so he was hired to repeat the trick at Dundarave.

Prince Edward Island is known for its red soil, red rocks, and red sand…even in bunkers. The 1st hole is a medium-length par 4 that is wide open and very large in scale, as are most of the other holes. Every hole is almost isolated from all the others by trees, wetlands, hills, or native areas, making each hole as peaceful as life itself on PEI.

The course does not have returning nines to the clubhouse, so the 10th hole is not really a starting hole, and hence can be a little more difficult. The fairway is wide but you must still avoid the bunkers if you hit it long. The second shot plays over a protected stream corridor, and then up to the green beyond. A 511-yard par 5, this hole is a good birdie possibility.

The Dundarave site was adjacent to the existing Brudenell River Golf Course in the Rodd's Brudenell River Resort. The total site was about 250 acres, with the ultimate plan of building a golf course and academy complex. The first step was to decide upon a clubhouse site, and one was selected to serve both the existing Brudenell River Course and the new Dundarave course. However this meant that the Dundarave course could not have returning nines because of space limitations. This turned out to be fortunate, for it meant the golf course could be routed further out onto the site, taking advantage of its most exciting parts.

The 16th is a good example of heroic design. At 332 yards long the hole is certainly driveable but that ultimate reward comes with extreme risk. The myriad of bunkers, built below grade, are deep and punishing, and if you happen to find one, recovery is rare. The hole can be played with two short irons by playing out to the wide fairway on the left, then deftly over the green side bunkers. Or, aim at the red flag, take a huge breath, hit it and hope.

The result is four distinct types of golf -- links, heathland, coastal and inland. Some golf holes play in open meadows, another section is in woods, a stretch winds along the river's edge, and several holes run up and down hills and skirt ponds and wetlands. The clay soils on PEI are made very red owing to their high iron content, and even the bunker sand is tainted red. Draining those clay soils became the biggest challenge and the most costly part of the construction. The contractor was an islander named Harry Annear, whose company, Kings County Construction, did a remarkable job interpreting our drawings, having patience with Robbie, and working in difficult site conditions.

There was one existing pond and wetland on the site, and it became a mild driving hazard on the 15th. From the blue markers it requires a 100-yard plus carry, but from the regular tees, average golfers can almost drive a ball into the right fairway bunker. From there, it is uphill and around the bend on this 467-yard par 4.

The favorite holes for some golfers will be the ones along the Brudenell River. For others, it will be the 17th, with its great long-range view from its very high tee. The scale of the property is huge and so are the tees, greens, fairways and especially the bunkers. The golf course is more reminiscent of an A.W. Tillinghast or Stanley Thompson style course than any other we've ever done. Some people will like that, and others will not. But it seems to fit the site.

———————————

One of the best views on PEI is from the par-3 17th tee, looking over the green down the 18th fairway and to the new clubhouse that serves both the Dundarave and Brudenell River courses. Just beyond the clubhouse is the Brudenell River, on which several holes of Dundarave play. Oh yes, when golfers on this tee finish sightseeing and return to golf, they face a 211-yard shot from the tips.

The par-5 18th finishes, by design, right in front of the new clubhouse. The old clubhouse can be seen off to the right, and beyond the pond to the right is the older Brudenell River course. Together, this is an exiting golf complex that fits perfectly in the reputation that PEI is building as a golf Mecca.

HOLE	PAR	YDS		HOLE	PAR	YDS
1	4	399		10	5	511
2	5	549		11	4	407
3	4	476		12	4	467
4	5	578		13	4	453
5	3	172		14	3	220
6	4	435		15	4	467
7	3	237		16	4	332
8	4	387		17	3	211
9	4	441		18	5	542
OUT	36	3674		IN	36	3610
				TOTAL	72	7284

©2002 Donald F. Keller

BRUDENELL RIVER

HURDZAN·FRY
·················
Great Golf by Design

Dundarave GC

Brudenell River Resort   Cardigan, PEI, Canada

The Dundarave site had lots of wonderful natural features to work with, including open meadows like on the 2nd hole, as well as woods, wetlands, streams, rivers, ponds, rocks and lots of room. Wherever possible, we left those natural features to blend into the more maintained golf course features such as on this 549-yard par 5.

Equally exciting to the golf course is the learning center, perhaps the finest in eastern Canada. An old barn was converted into an indoor practice range for those months when everything on PEI is frozen except thoughts of improving the golf swing. Then there is a huge outdoor, natural grass practice range tee that will always have good turf on it, with a private teaching tee at the far end. The short game center (or centre, as Canadians spell it) is the place to learn and practice all kinds of approach shots from twenty yards out. These facilities are complimented with two large putting greens and a very enjoyable 9-hole executive golf course. Anyone who is even slightly thinking about learning to play golf, or play better, will find the opportunity at the Canadian Golf Academy.

Even with the new bridge, Prince Edward Island is not easy to get to, and perhaps that is one reason it is so special. Once there you will want to return, again and again.

That flag is not starched. That's simply how hard the wind blows off the Brudenell River. Looking back toward the various tees on the par-3 5th hole, you can only guess how close to the river you must aim to allow for the wind. Even on warm, windless days, the hole is still a 172-yard long shot from the back tee.

The setting for the 9th hole, when one looks back 441 yards towards the tee, is the tidal Brudenell River, and the ocean is only a short distance beyond. Not only are the river views incredible it is close enough to be in play, as are the winds that sweep across it. Playing this par 4 hole alone is worth the trip to PEI.

You may think of Delaware for its many contributions to early American history, and as the home of DuPont, but certainly not for having steep hills and hard rocky ledges. When we were first invited to the site of Fieldstone by its founders, Buddy Reed and Dr. Barry Roseman, we expected nice rolling farm fields and deep rich topsoil. Those must be in some other part of the state. But what we found instead didn't disappoint us.

Perhaps if we hadn't done so many mountain golf courses by that time, we might have labeled the site as "impossible." Instead, we labeled it "expensive." One great truth of course design we've learned over the years is that the more difficult the site is to work with, the more spectacular will be the finished product. We knew the Fieldstone site would produce an incredible golf course. Buddy and Barry thought so too, but they were seeing it from a player's perspective. We approached it as designers who had to make things work.

Buddy is a fixture in Delaware golf, has played in every important tournament in the region, and has been considered one of the area's leading amateurs. These guys know golf and golf courses. They knew exactly what they wanted - a first class member's club on land owned by Mrs. Lisa Moseley, a member of the DuPont family.

The routing was done by our associate David Whelchel, who found the one and only possible way to get in both returning nines and a practice range, even if it was going to take a little rock-blasting and a lot of earthmoving to make things work. The clubhouse is nicely located atop the highest hill, with spectacular views of the pristine Delaware countryside and golf holes below.

Even though a golfer's second shot to the par-4 15th green must carry a pond built from a deep valley, it is still a fun and fair shot. The pond is narrow along the right side and there is lots of room to miss a shot short or right of the pond or green. However, the left rear hole locations are a different story on this 439-yard hole.

Fieldstone's routing builds in suspense and tension the farther into each nine you play, with the individual character of each hole determined by what was there when we started. The par-5 second hole is carved into a hillside that narrows as it gets closer to the green, thus placing a greater value on accuracy the longer the golfer hits it. It's a classic risk-and- reward strategy that just happens to occur naturally. The tees for the fourth hole are perfectly positioned on one hilltop and the landing area on another. The two are separated by a 60-foot deep valley. It takes only a 180-yard carry to reach the fairway, but it looks much, much longer. The par-3 sixth hole plays downhill some 90 feet. The par-3 eighth is positioned in a valley, with ponds, waterfalls and a hillside backdrop.

The long par-5 10th is narrow, well bunkered and plays 607 yards. It's uphill almost 30 feet from the landing area to the green, making it one of the toughest par 5's without a water hazard you'll likely play. Rarely does any golfer get home in two, so eagles are rare.

The 13th green was benched into a hillside, with a deep ravine separating the tees and green. There is plenty of room to bail out to the left, the shortest distance across the ravine. It takes a bold, well hit shot of 219 yards to attack any hole location on the right rear part of the green.

Dana is a master at balancing colors, shapes and textures to produce golf holes that look awesome from the tee. The par-3 16th hole looks more like it is set in an English countryside, given the stone wall and stone clubhouse, than on a Delaware farm. The hole is a short 130 yards.

Great golf courses, like great stories, have dramatic endings, and Fieldstone is a fine example. The home hole is 524 yards long, uphill to a well-contoured green, with bunkers on all sides and a small menacing one in front.

Not many people think of Delaware as being steep or rocky, but on this site it was both. All of the stone used in the walls and clubhouse came from the site. Beyond the downhill 17th you get a glimpse of distant hills. Few folks would recognize this course as being near Wilmington, Delaware.

HOLE	PAR	YDS	HOLE	PAR	YDS
1	4	442	10	5	607
2	5	579	11	4	304
3	3	182	12	4	369
4	4	354	13	3	219
5	5	530	14	4	476
6	3	184	15	4	439
7	4	347	16	3	130
8	3	183	17	4	436
9	4	443	18	5	524
OUT	35	3244	IN	36	3504
			TOTAL	71	6748

©2002 Donald F. Keller

HURDZAN · FRY
Great Golf by Design

Talk about intimidating drives, how about the 7th? This photo is from the senior tee. A forward tee is on the fairway side of the ravine. Although the fairway is narrow, it plays quite wide for left to right shots. The 7th is a short 347 yards from the pro tee, so anything on the fairway is a short iron approach.

The setting for the 4th green feels like it's at the end of the earth because of the super steep drop offs in three directions. It took massive amounts of rock blasting and earthmoving to build this hole, but the end result speaks for itself. Just 354 yards, it is a difficult driving hole, but if you reach the driving area. It is a short iron to the green.

––––––––––––

What people may remember most at this fine club are not the natural elements, but the manmade ones. The clubhouse was designed in the style of a farmhouse and it seems to fit the site so perfectly that it feels as if it's been there forever. It feels quaint and snug, but is really quite large in its square footage. There are the several manmade ponds on the course, adding much diversity to the site. The foundations of homesteads of early settlers were preserved and integrated into play areas. But probably the most distinguishing feature are the dry-stacked fieldstone walls that Buddy and Barry had built throughout the property. These walls add an Old Country color and texture to the golfscape.

A dramatic forested hillside, rock-lined waterfalls, a pond, a large green and a couple of small bunkers are the design elements of the par-3 8th. The under story beneath the trees has been planted to laurels and azaleas, so in the spring there will be a celebration of color.

Stonewalls were also used to support tee slopes, define boundaries, establish backdrops for some greens and occasionally even to serve as hazards. There is a strength and direction to the walls that seem to reflect the value of golf itself.

Of all of the golf courses done by Hurdzan/Fry, none more reflects the character and sense of its location than does Fieldstone.

A photograph can't convey just how dramatic this terrain really is. It is about a 90-foot drop to the green on the par-3 6th hole, and any shot that lands on the steep back slope, and doesn't go in a bunker, will generally bound back on the green. The stone wall in the background separates the 6th and 7th holes.

It is not unusual for a golf course site to have historic ruins on it, but it is rare when the ruins can be worked into the strategy of a hole or two. This foundation of an early 19th century house separates the play areas on the 12th and 14th holes (along with some sod-faced pot bunkers). The 12th plays to the left of the foundation to the green, and the 14th plays from the tees to the right.

The Heritage
GOLF COURSE AT WESTMOOR

The Denver suburb of Westminster is a vibrant and dynamic community with a good balance of residential, commercial and public areas. The city management consists of free-thinking innovators who want to preserve traditional values but keep their community on the leading edge of progress. This attitude attracted a large development company that saw value in producing an upscale office park around an equally upscale public golf course. A public-private partnership deal was struck. The developer would build the office park and deed the adjacent land to the city on the stipulation that the city would build and operate a golf course.

For years, Hurdzan/Fry had tried to get a project in Colorado without success. So when we were asked to interview for the Westminster project we poured our heart and soul into the proposal, interview, and follow-up process. We had the talent, history and the commitment to do the job, and it must have showed, for we were selected. Then began a very different kind of golf course planning challenge for us, of integrating a golf course within a large office park complex while also respecting wetlands, flood plains, some ancient trees, some dramatic topography and a couple of prairie dog towns.

_____

The full name of the golf course is The Heritage Golf Course at Westmoor, and does the place ever resemble a moor. The golf course was routed to leave as much native plant material as possible between the holes, and the irrigation system was designed so as not to water them and change their character. This view from behind the 9th green, across the 1st green, and onto the 5th green shows the results of this effort.

Most people would be surprised at the amount of civil engineering that goes into planning a golf course. When you immerse it into an officepark, it takes even more planners and engineers, each concerned with different details, all needing to be coordinated. Some course design firms simply subcontract an engineer for the golf course issues, but unless the engineer understands the art of golf course design they often propose solutions that negatively impact the golf course. Hurdzan/Fry is perhaps uniquely qualified because our associate Bill Kerman is a civil engineer by training and experience, and a golf course architect by choice. Early on, it was decided that Bill would have principal responsibility for this project, and it paid

The open, sprawling nature of the course provides for wonderful color contrasts particularly at sunrise and sunset. The par-5 18th hole borders a large pond providing both a visually dramatic and strategically challenging conclusion to a round at The Heritage.

big dividends to the course, the city and the developer. Bill is a master of finding engineering-based solutions to big problems and presenting them in such a way as to look like featured assets of a course. Such problems as storm water retention, roadway alignment, utility line locations, and even an irrigation canal bisecting the property can be unsightly on a golf course. Bill deftly handled all those problems yet modified them to look attractive. As you will see when you play the back nine at The Heritage at Westmoor, Bill camouflaged them well.

The perfect clubhouse location was right next to the irrigation canal, but that was also to be bordered by a four-lane entrance boulevard. The easy solution would have been to move the clubhouse, but that would have compromised the routing of the golf course, so Bill and the planning team decided to pipe the canal in a tunnel under the clubhouse and parking lot. That sounds like a simple task, but far from it. It was the perfect solution, though, that preserved the routing, the clubhouse location, and even the canal.

⋀ *One of the greatest visual differences of how golfers react to a golf hole is light. They seldom get to see the same hole in two different sun angles during the same round. At high light angles your eye tends to scan the broad landscape while at low light angles, as in the picture, you focus more on the highlighting and shadowing of the features. The 4th hole itself measures 230 yards, but with the Colorado altitude and the prevailing wind at your back, the hole plays much shorter.*

≺ *The golf course is owned by the City of Westminster and the new community / recreation center adjoins the golf course. Walking trails from the center are integrated within the golf course, but golfers and walkers are safely separated. Between the 5th hole and the community center, dinosaur fossils were discovered and preserved during construction – hence the dinosaur logo for the golf course.*

The par-3 14th hole is the highest part of the golf course. While the shortest hole on the course, the broad panorama of open plains and the distant mountains provides for confusing depth perception so club selection is tricky. Wind is always a factor on this course, but nowhere more than on this short and scenic hole.

HOLE	PAR	YDS	HOLE	PAR	YDS
1	4	392	10	4	421
2	4	434	11	4	361
3	5	570	12	4	466
4	3	230	13	5	595
5	4	451	14	3	163
6	5	521	15	4	494
7	3	200	16	4	451
8	4	411	17	3	229
9	4	390	18	5	566
OUT	36	3599	IN	36	3746
			TOTAL	72	7345

The Heritage GC
at Westmoor   Westminster, Colorado

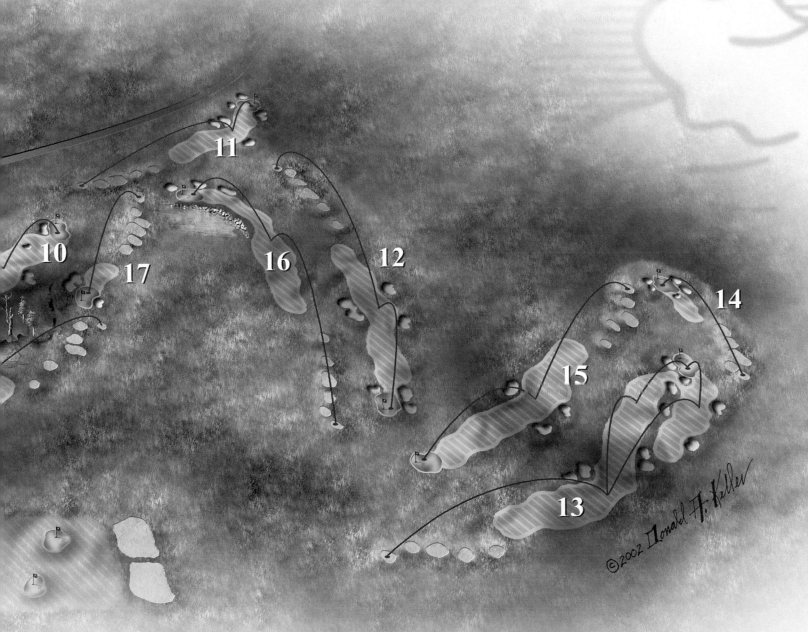

11

10

17

16

12

14

15

13

©2002 Donald F. Keller

HURDZAN · FRY

Great Golf by Design

The front nine at Heritage starts across the boulevard and down the hill from the clubhouse with a dramatic mountain backdrop. This yielded a wonderful mix of holes that cross creeks and wetlands, along the edge of relocated prairie dog towns, up and down gentle hills, past a couple of specimen trees and back up to a spectacular ninth hole with a great high hillside as the backdrop. The back nine zigzags its way across an open prairie and up a huge hill, culminating with the nearly 600 yard par 5 13th hole.

To appreciate the setting of a golf course you often need to look at the course from more than the eye of the golfer as they play a hole – such is the case at The Heritage. Looking back up the 6th hole and across the 8th hole, the Front Range of the Rocky Mountains provides a constant backdrop to the course.

The few trees that are on the site are along the Walnut Creek. The setting of the eighth green takes advantage of one of these tree groups to frame the green. When Mike Hurdzan and Bill Kerman first visited the site, this location was picked as a green site almost immediately upon starting their first site walk. They did not yet know how the rest of the routing would evolve, but they knew there would be a green in this location.

Y ou can try to catch your breath at the 14th tee but it isn't easy, for not only is the short par 3 a dramatic hole, but the views from the top of the hill are breathtaking. To the west are the foothills, with the snow-capped Rocky Mountains beyond. In another direction is the City of Westminster and its distinctive clock tower, and beyond that the skyline of downtown Denver.

On the golf course, verdant green fairways flow through great expanses of golden brown native grasses. While the fairways are wide, the ever present, but varying winds, provide a constantly changing, challenging golf course each day you can play. We couldn't have asked for a better way to introduce our firm to the citizens of the Colorado area than The Heritage at Westmoor.

The Walnut Creek meanders through the front nine until reaching the pond at the 7th hole, a challenging par 3. While the pond may look intimidating, there is room to bail out to the right and front of the green. This pond is part of a protected open water and wetland complex and was enhanced in accordance with the Audubon International golf course certification standards.

The River Course
AT KEYSTONE

Many years back, I visited a sports trade show and met Steve Corneillier, an impressive young guy representing the Keystone Ski area. We got to talking about their award-winning Keystone Ranch Golf Course. Like most ski areas, Keystone had recognized that adding golf to its summer amenity package would foster the image of a four-season resort, not just a winter vacation spot. Vacation housing that sits idle during the summer makes no sense or cents. However if you can offer summer activities, people will rent the condos in June and July. Keystone offered horseback riding, hiking, biking, climbing, canoeing, fishing, and lots of other fun things to do, but they figured out it's golf that attracts the affluent buyer. So they built Keystone Ranch in the late 1970s.

Over the years, Steve and I would run into one another, but I never thought we'd someday work together developing another course at Keystone. But in 1996, after a rigorous selection process, we found ourselves doing our first ski area golf course, The River Course at Keystone. It came with a whole new set of challenges to make it interesting. To begin with, the site was bounded on one side by State Highway 6 (which runs to Keystone from Interstate 70), on another by a horse meadow (which became a major public relations nightmare), on another by a housing development (which became a legal nightmare), and on the final side by a mountain range (which became an earthmoving nightmare). Through the middle of the site flowed the open-access, but very protected, trout stream called the Snake River, along with a giant steel-tower electric transmission line and an ancient winter migration corridor for elk.

As you play the 519-yard uphill par-5 13th hole, your thoughts and eyes are on the golfing tasks at hand. But once you complete this fascinating hole, and you move up towards the next tee, you might glance back over your shoulder and catch one of the prettiest scenes in golf. The middle ground is Lake Dillon and some of its surrounding development. Beyond are the mountains known as The Gore Range. Buffalo Mountain is the rounded one to the left.

The Keystone real estate developers which owned the land, had development rights for housing units in the middle of the parcel, on the most gentle land (worth about 25 million dollars). To further complicate things, the local fire chief set an elevation limit at which he could provide fire protection. That severely restricted the location of a clubhouse. So the land we were given for the golf course was mostly very steep terrain.

Permitting was complicated, public hearings were both numerous and contentious, and public scrutiny was intense. With so many problems, I doubted if the project would ever get permitted. But it did, and in spite of all the compromises that had to be made, the golf course turned out to be outstanding.

Most visitors do not really think about mountains changing colors until they see photos such as this one taken from 15 green. Notice how different the blues of the water in Lake Dillon and the sky are, and how purple the mountains are. Seeing it first hand may even make you think that the person who wrote the lyrics for "America the Beautiful" that speaks of "...purple mountain majesty..." was a mountain golfer.

Much is made of golf courses built on the tops of mountains. Even though they provide unencumbered 360° views, the golf holes usually lack a backdrop to make them interesting. But courses built in valley areas are usually looking up into the mountains. The par-3 12th hole has very simple, low-profile shaping, made memorable by the trees and mountains in the background. Your eyes move upward, where earth and heaven are merged into one.

Golf course design is a complex process. Each site seems to favor a different set of skills, technical knowledge and experience to artistically solve all the problems. At Keystone, the most important element was the routing plan, and no one is more masterful at routing plans than our associate Bill Kerman. His civil engineer training also benefits us, for there are usually lots of engineering issues to be considered in routing a course.

In spring and early fall, when there is snow on the higher elevations, and you are on a lush green golf course, you are reminded what a land of contrasts this is and how every season is special in its own way. The view from behind the 14th green is back to the Continental Divide near Loveland Pass and the start of Ten Mile Range. All a designer needs to do on such sites is to make them playable, and nature will add the "wow" factor.

Typically, uphill par 3's are difficult to design and not much fun to play. The 15th hole on The River Course is an exception, maybe because it offers a large diagonal green with only a couple of bunkers to provide the challenge. Or perhaps because, while waiting your turn to putt you will get a great view of Buffalo Mountain just right of the tee and you forget about everything except how lucky you are to be there.

At the time, Bill was single and an avid skier, so he didn't mind spending days and days out on the site, to find the best and most practical solutions. I remember several winter visits, on snowshoes, in the bitter cold, trying to confirm an engineering detail or observe the elk migration. Bill loved it.

Despite all its problems, the site for The River Course at Keystone had lots of assets, especially in the eye and mind of a golf course designer. We saw a wonderfully diverse landscape of high hills, awe-inspiring mountain views, great trees, huge boulders, a rippling mountain stream and decent soils. It also helped that we were working with a strong planning and development team that knew how to set reasonable budgets and spend money wisely. Another plus was that the housing would be placed in a core area, rather than spread throughout the golf course.

There are few opening tee shots more spectacular then the one on the 1st hole at The River Course. The fairway is 90-feet below the tee on this short par 5, framed by trees and mountainsides. Here bunkers were put in to define shot values as well as guide the eye and turn the hole toward the green some 551 yards away.

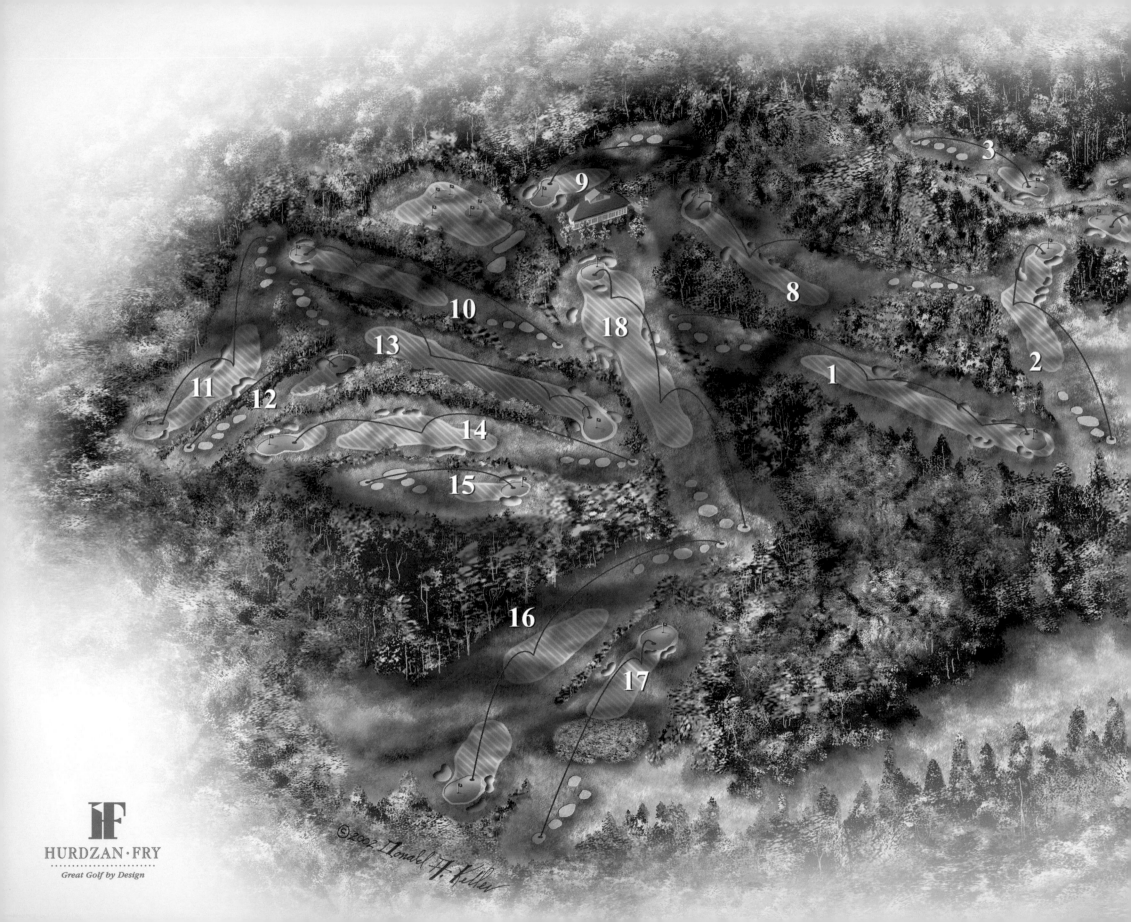

The River Course

at Keystone   Keystone, Colorado

HOLE	PAR	YDS	HOLE	PAR	YDS
1	5	551	10	4	408
2	4	397	11	4	415
3	3	222	12	3	209
4	4	408	13	5	519
5	5	563	14	4	441
6	4	363	15	3	184
7	3	195	16	4	509
8	4	431	17	4	330
9	3	221	18	5	520
OUT	35	3351	IN	36	3535
			TOTAL	71	6886

The importance of contrasts, shades and shadows is clearly demonstrated on of the par-4 16th. Notice how the shadows on the bunkers contrast with the white sand to help define their depth, how the dark green shade in the trees contrasts with the light green color of the putting surface, and how the off-color native grasses outside the rough line accent it. These are results of conscious design decisions.

A *The finishing hole on The River Course was one of the first holes decided upon in the planning phase for lots of reasons, but none more important than because it was a spectacular way to end a round. The drive from the tee drops about 140 feet to a generous fairway, leaving an uphill second to another large landing area beyond the bunkers on this par 5 of 520 yards. After an accurate approach, the round ends with a great view of Lake Dillon and The Gore Range.*

Finally (and I mean, finally), a routing plan was conceived that satisfied almost everyone's' objectives and objections, and construction was approved. At the 9,500-foot elevation, the construction and growing season is short, so enormous efforts were made during that narrow window of time to complete the course on time and on budget. Construction actually began in the early spring, with the clearing of trees while the snow base was still several feet deep. Mountain summer temperatures range from 25° to 85°, depending on the month and time of day, but with little rainfall, most every day is a good working day for golf course construction.

During the first year of construction, our bosses at Keystone Real Estate Development said that whatever else we did, we must have the eighth hole complete and looking like a golf hole by early July 1998 for a big real estate sales weekend. We succeeded in turning a rock quarry into a golf hole in 45 days by sodding the entire hole. As predicted, it was a busy weekend. House lots were sold by lottery, with each buyer securing a spot in the lottery by posting a $5,000 security. When a buyer's turn arose, he'd get 30 minutes to select a lot from what remained.

Mornings and evenings, when the sun is low and shadows are long, the golf course takes on an ethereal quality. This view of the second landing area on the 18th looks markedly different now than when the sun is well up. Such times on a golf course become burned into a golfer's memory and last a lifetime.

I was later told that lot sales for the weekend were over 20 million dollars. And buyers were basically seeing just one golf hole of the entire course.

Working with Steve, his first assistant Craig Belcher (later to become the first course superintendent), and the rest of the team was pure pleasure. There were problems and squabbles, but none overshadowed the enjoyment of working in that environment with experienced and savvy people. The golf course is a testament to that cooperation.

From the drive off the first tee to a fairway 90 feet below, with the Rocky Mountains as a backdrop, to the last drive, which drops about 140 feet to the fairway, and has Lake Dillon and The Gore Range as the setting, The River Course at Keystone is an exciting and stimulating round of golf. The holes play up and down changes in elevation, but the course is surprisingly walkable for a fairly fit golfer. The routing takes us beside the Snake River and across it, through stands of beautiful old Douglas fir and birch, past boulders, rock walls and to vantage points that offer great views. In the winter, the course is used by cross-country skiers and snow shoe enthusiasts. And the elk happily play through. Just as they've done for centuries.

The Snake River is a protected stream that flows through the site and is part of the strategy on the par-3 7th hole, especially from the back where it measures 195 yards. Protecting and using such streams is an important part of intelligent golf course design. In this case, the stream feels like part of the hole despite the wide buffers on both sides of it.

Huntsville, Alabama is a thriving community due in large part to its proximity to the U.S. Army Redstone Arsenal and the U.S. Space and Rocket Center. Huntsville's historic district contains over 65 homes built prior to the 1860s, and legend has it the invading Civil War troops thought they were so beautiful that they left them untouched.

Although Huntsville is immensely proud of its history and tradition, the city is also eager to embrace new ideas and technology as well as new residents and visitors. The area is growing, and they love golf, but there hadn't been a new first-class country club built there in decades. In the late 1990s, Huntsville was ripe for a new golf course, but with golf courses there is no such thing as spontaneous generation. It takes a person to plant the seed, and a group of people to nurture the idea, put up the funds and grow the idea to fruition.

Fortunately for Huntsville there was John Blue and his family, who owned a large farm and part of a monolith known as Huntsville Mountain. The Ledges development encompassed over 750 acres. On top of the mountain was over 225 acres of beautiful, gently rolling woods and scenic 360° views of the surrounding valleys nearly 1,000 feet below. The reason the ground was still undeveloped was because it was "dag gum hard" to get up there. But in typical Huntsville spirit, the Blues knew they could find a way to the mountaintop, even if it meant rearranging the mountain a little.

The golf course and Smart Growth housing community are built on a relatively flat mountaintop of about 225 acres. It's almost a 1,000-foot drop into the valley below down all sides of this plateau. Not only is the air a little fresher and cooler up here in the summer, the views off the mountain are spectacular in any season and at any time, day or night. This view is from the 14th green.

The Ledges was an easy name to decide upon, and the reason why can be seen in this view of the 437-yard 2nd, a dogleg-left that hugs some high, sheer natural rock faces. The golf course was routed to put most of these drop-offs on the left, since average golfers tend to slice it right. Better players, who tend to hook, find the ledge holes very challenging.

I've said before, there are often engineering issues that profoundly shape a golf course routing. Three crucial ones are access road, clubhouse location and irrigation source. At The Ledges of Huntsville Mountain, it took an enormous amount of engineering and construction to create the fabulous 2.5-mile-long approach road up a steep mountain slope. It took even more know-how to be able to find a water source in the valley and pump water up 950' of elevation to an enormous water tank. Selecting the clubhouse location and the dozens of home sites for the retro village-style development was comparatively easy, but not without some difficult decisions. One dilemma was whether to place the homes along the top rim of the mountain, to offer homeowners some spectacular long range views, and place the golf course in the interior, or build the golf holes along the super-valuable edge-of-the-cliff settings and position the housing in the interior of the site.

Even rock cliffs sometimes need help to remain stable and yield enough room for a reasonable landing area. The fence is obviously here to warn cart drivers, but it also serves to accent the stone work. The result is the 8th hole, beautiful to look at and fun to play, unless you hook your tee shot on this 590-yard par 5, or your second, or your third…

Just short of the landing area on the 16th one can see how offsetting the fairway bunkers narrows the margin of error for long hitters, but doesn't affect average golfers. All golfers get treated the same though, when it comes to carrying their second shot over the 10-foot-deep sod wall bunker. Admittedly, it is only a mid or short-iron shot, but it is full of suspense.

Since there was no practical way to compromise, John Blue and his investors decided to build the golf course out on the ledges. This resulted in some awe-inspiring golf holes. And the home sites still offer some great panoramas, over both the golf holes and the countryside beyond.

As we routed the golf course, our emphasis was to place the slice-side of most holes away from the cliffs. That means better players, who usually hook the ball, must worry about launching one off the mountaintop.

Small wet low spots were really not large or complex enough to be called wetlands by traditional standards. However, they did provide some important habitat sustainment functions, were attractive to look at, and were part of the overall site drainage, so we decided to keep and enhance them. This little one on 13 is out-of-play but still adds character.

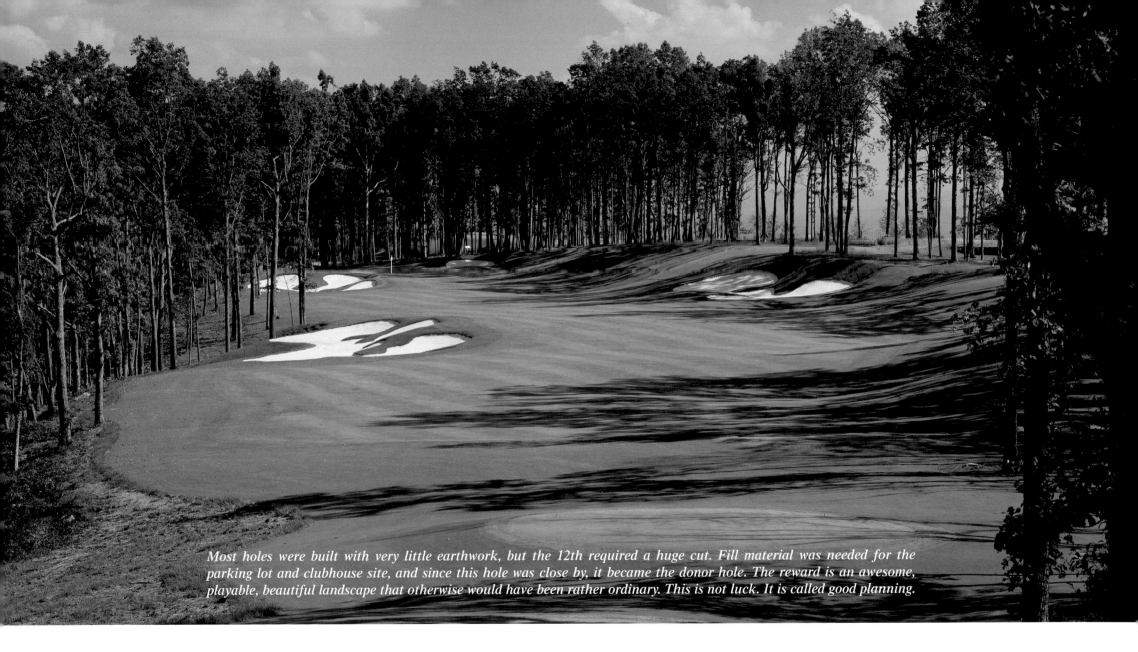

Most holes were built with very little earthwork, but the 12th required a huge cut. Fill material was needed for the parking lot and clubhouse site, and since this hole was close by, it became the donor hole. The reward is an awesome, playable, beautiful landscape that otherwise would have been rather ordinary. This is not luck. It is called good planning.

There were lots of nice mature trees to separate the village homes from the golf course, and best of all there was lots of nice topsoil. The topsoil was a surprise, for everywhere we looked, we saw rocks the size of small houses and sheer rock cliffs. Initially, we thought we'd have to truck topsoil up the mountain, which would have cost a million dollars or more. But since we found plenty of soil already up there, we took this as a sign that the caddy master in the sky had pre-selected this as golf course site. So our task was to design a course to play around the rocks and cliffs, taking advantage of their assets, keeping as many trees as possible, and making the golf course walkable. We succeeded on all counts except for a cart shuttle that carries walking golfers up a long hill from the sixth green to the seventh tee.

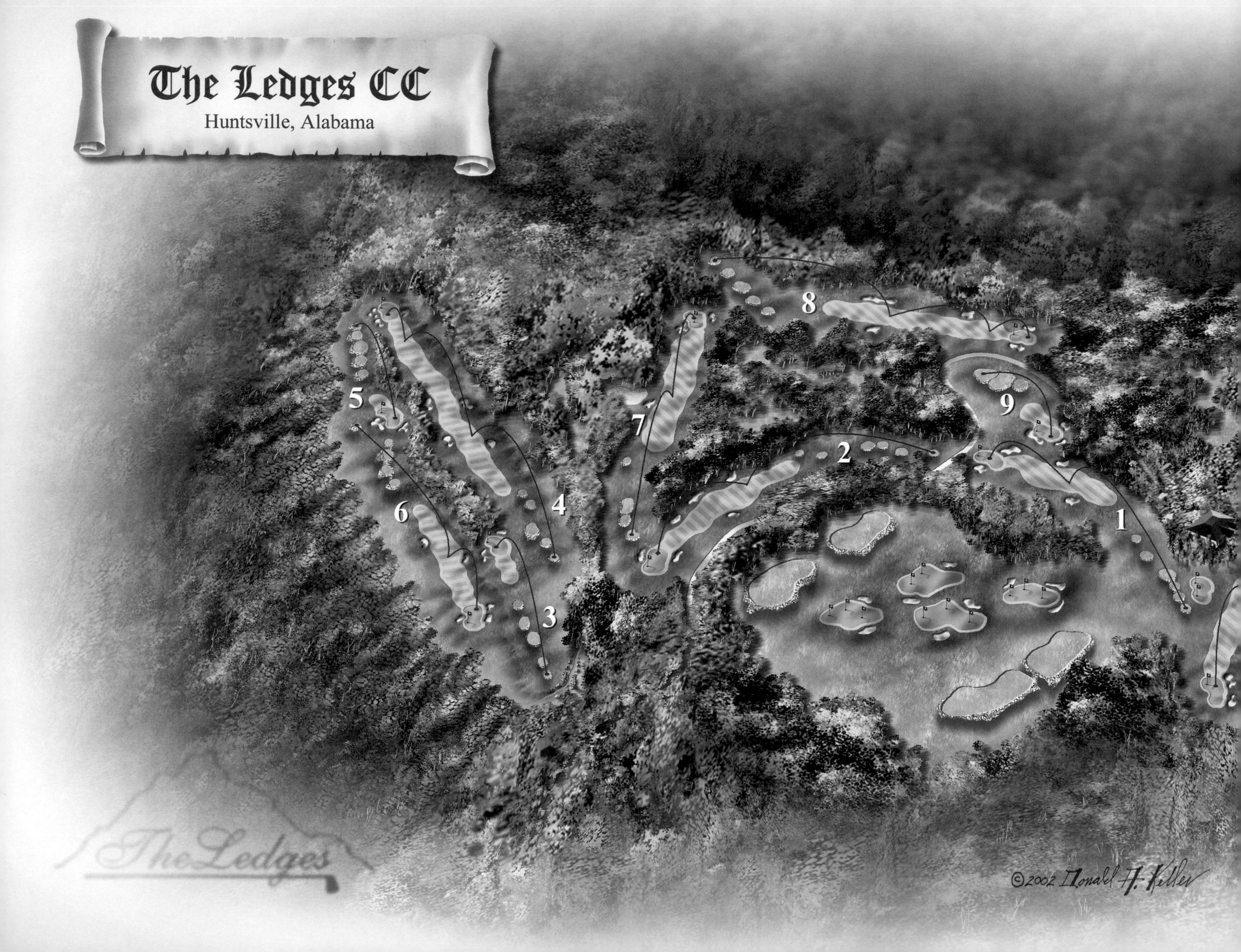

The Ledges CC

Huntsville, Alabama

©2002 Donald H. Keller

HOLE	PAR	YDS	HOLE	PAR	YDS
1	4	436	10	5	568
2	4	437	11	3	203
3	3	201	12	4	405
4	5	614	13	3	218
5	3	183	14	4	449
6	4	461	15	5	519
7	4	446	16	4	406
8	5	590	17	4	409
9	3	191	18	4	464
OUT	35	3559	IN	36	3641
			TOTAL 71		7200

The Ledges was designed in the timeless style of raised tees, wide fairways, large undulating greens, simply-shaped bunkers and almost no gimmicks. One notable exception to the traditional design theme was Dana's idea to put a 10-foot-deep sod-wall bunker in front of the 16th green.

Despite its old-style look, The Ledges incorporates the latest and best technology available. The turfgrasses are improved cultivars of bent greens, zoysia fairways and Bermuda roughs that can take the heat of summer, are pest resistant and require low fertilizer and water applications. Several greens have underground air pumps, which can remove excess moisture from the root zone when needed, or pump in cool air to relieve stress on the roots. The state-of-the-art irrigation system allows precise applications of precious water resources. Course superintendent Jim Howell, formerly at Tavern Creek in Missouri, had previous success growing grass on an Alabama golf course. There's nothing more critical to a golf course than a well-trained, experienced golf course superintendent. Give him or her the latest technology and a membership willing to fund top quality maintenance, and the playing conditions can be awesome.

Understandably, when one designs on top of a mountain, there is some expectation that rock may be a problem. On holes like the 2nd, the rock had to be drilled and blasted, which added to the expense, but also added a unique look to the course.

Four holes had to be built down from the mountaintop, on side slopes of pure rock. Most of that rock was large but loose because it had fallen down from higher elevations. One of the worst areas was used for the par-3 5th hole, where much of the out-of-play rock was retained for accent. The 6th hole can be seen beyond five green.

The par-5 10th hole is a pretty hole anytime, but in the evening, when long shadows cross the fairway and sunlight highlights the green and bunker, it takes on special qualities. The rock edged pond was part of an existing, slowly-draining low area that was expanded and stabilized to provide better habitat support. The front green bunker is much deeper and menacing than it looks, so getting home in two is a challenge on this 568-yard hole.

Our intent at The Ledges was to let the site speak for itself by creating a place that would allow golfers to relax and enjoy the entire experience, unless they have an uncontrollable hook. Those golfers might consider just going for the scenery.

———

The entire theme of The Ledges is of the friendly formality commonly associated with genuine southern hospitality. This honest but direct approach can even be seen in the construction and landscaping of the tees on the par-3 13th hole. It is elegant in its simplicity, yet reminds the golfer of how much pride the members take in the place, and how special the golf course is.

CONCORD, OHIO

It may be an exaggeration to call one of the highest points in northeast Ohio a Little Mountain, for it is only about 400 feet higher than Lake Erie some five miles away. The name actually came from settlers in the late 1700s, because from one spot in particular (now the 17th tee), they could see Lake Erie. So the name stuck.

But it's no exaggeration to call Little Mountain Country Club one of Hurdzan/Fry's proudest works. Not only for the quality of the golf experience, but also for the problems overcome in getting it constructed.

The 300-acre tract some 30 miles east of Cleveland was characterized by rolling land bisected by 60-foot-deep stream corridors eroded into the land since the last glacier. The area was mostly tree covered, soils were thin, interspersed with overlaid shale rock. The land had a sort of untouched feeling to it, even though years ago it had been cleared and farmed, then allowed to re-grow into forest. It served as a hunting and shooting preserve for its last owners.

The bunkers in the foreground help define and protect the prime left side driving area on the 13th hole. A well-placed drive here risks the steep embankment to the left but reduces the danger for the second shot. Playing away from the embankment to the right causes golfers to aim right at it on their second shots. Golfers need all of the help they can get on this 487-yard par 4.

Along the margins of Lake Erie, a predominant tree is the beech, which lose their leaves early in the fall, as can be seen in this photo of the 471-yard par-4 10th. The area to the left of the fairway drops about 60 feet to a protected creek valley below. Several holes like this one, snug up very close to the edge, making it interesting for golfers who hook the ball. Notice the colorful maple trees growing on this bank.

A local engineer had done a residential golf course plan for the property, and on the basis of that plan the project had been surveyed and deeded. When we got involved, lots were already being sold and some golf course corridors had been cleared. As the golf course superintendent wasn't comfortable with the tightness of the plan, he had suggested the owners get a second opinion, particularly with regard to the closeness of golf holes to house lots. The other designer had apparently applied an older safety standard for housing separation that today is not considered safe. So we were hired to salvage the course.

Simple, small, fairly shallow bunkers define the ➤ *play area and set shot value on the dogleg left 5th hole. From the tee on this 413-yard hole, the golfer must play right of the bunker in the fairway, leaving a second shot over a front green bunker, or play left of the fairway bunker, risking a very deep bunker nicknamed 'Grand Canyon of the East' inside the dogleg, but resulting in an easy approach shot.*

The 3rd hole is only 366 yards long and plays downhill to a landing area that ends at a small, deep, rock-lined creek. From there it is a short or medium iron approach to an elevated green with the creek hugging its right side. The bunkers are more for shot containment and direction than strategic elements.

White silica sand is mined very close to Little Mountain, so it is much less expensive and we used more on this course than others. The 11th has two fairways, a narrow upper one that opens up the approach angle into the green, and the wide lower fairway to the left. What makes the risk and reward strategy work is the dramatic use of bunkers on this 369-yard hole.

Golf course safety is the number one planning issue in our firm. We spend a great deal of time studying and applying practical safety guidelines. The challenge at Little Mountain was that the course was on too small of a piece of land. It was trapped between the deep, legally-protected creek valleys, an already-plotted-and-constructed road system and already-sold housing lots. We convinced the golf course developer to hold back some home lots to allow for a proper golf course. We had to dramatically change the original routing, yet get it to fit into areas already cleared as fairways.

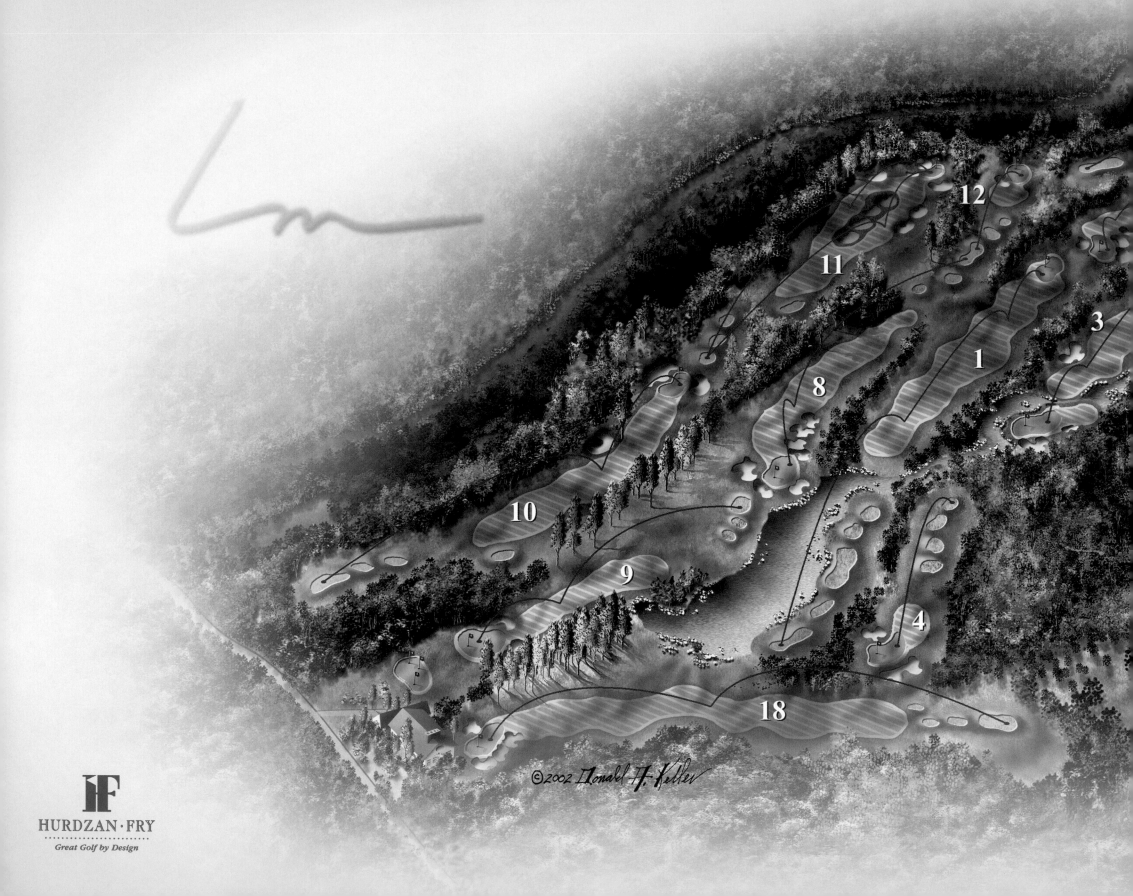

Little Mountain CC

Concord, Ohio

HOLE	PAR	YDS
1	5	582
2	3	148
3	4	366
4	3	197
5	4	413
6	3	234
7	5	524
8	4	341
9	4	401
OUT	35	3206
10	4	471
11	4	369
12	3	135
13	4	487
14	3	155
15	4	373
16	4	387
17	5	552
18	4	481
IN	35	3410
TOTAL	70	6616

Our associate Jason Straka was given the task of finding the solutions. He routed it so that most fairways border the deep creek valleys on the left side of the holes. That makes Little Mountain fun to play if you slice or fade the ball, which most average golfers do, while highly skilled golfers find it a bit intimidating, especially if they can't control a right-to-left shot. That's the way a great golf course should play.

But the sheer drop-offs on the left of several holes are just one feature. Equally interesting are the series of ponds and creeks created in the natural drainage passageways that supply the irrigation pond. As the land had great contours, the course has a nice balance of uphill and downhill holes. Jason and Dana accented these features with thoughtful bunker placement, producing a strategic-concept course that offers lots of ways to play each hole.

Even though this is an early morning photograph with long shadows, it does not really show all the undulation that shapes and defines the par-3 14th. As you might imagine, the left-side hole locations are the most demanding on this short 155-yard hole.

Pioneers supposedly gave the name Little Mountain to the hillside that now holds the 552-yard 17th hole. In the distance you can see Lake Erie, which is a pretty rare sight because most of northeast Ohio is not very high above it. The foreground is the second landing area on this par 5 for average golfers, while long hitters can carry the cross bunkers and maybe roll on to the green. Beyond the 17th is the 18th hole that sits in a hillside below the clubhouse.

A huge oak tree serves as the backdrop for ➤ the green on the short par-3 12th. The green is a plateau that falls off to the left and the back, and the left front bunker puts a premium on flying the ball all 135 yards onto the putting surface. Just as troubling is the hill on the right front of the green that usually stops shots that miss the open front of the green.

There are many people important to this project who, for various reasons, came and went. Two mainstays throughout were Tom Scheetz, the course superintendent, and Jimmy Hanlin, the director of golf. Tom had previous construction experience with us as an assistant superintendent at StoneWater, on Cleveland's east side, and Jimmy had been at a resort that had recently added a golf course. These guys constantly solved day-to-day problems that could have slowed or delayed the project, and lent their ideas and expertise during construction and grow-in. They faced countless problems, from major storm damage to coordinating sub-contractors to occasional weak financing. The finished course testifies to how well we all worked as a team.

The course now has a new owner who sees the real potential for the course and is already instituting improvements thought too costly by the original developers. Little Mountain literally rises above most other golf courses in this golf-rich region of Ohio. I predict, someday soon, it will do so figuratively as well.

_____

From the 8th tee, golfers can see Lake Erie on the horizon, but their attention is more likely drawn to the water of the irrigation pond behind and left of the green, and to the heavy bunkering around the driving area and green. Beyond the green is the 9th fairway. Despite all of the sand and water on 8, it plays rather easy as it is a reachable par 4 of 341 yards.

Hamilton Farm is a 730-acre estate in the upscale central New Jersey community of Bedminster Township, only a few miles from the U.S. Golf Association's headquarters. The entry drive from the front gate to the center of the property is like something out The Great Gatsby. You expect to pass Duesenbergs and Phaetons as the road winds through horse meadows, across stone bridges, over babbling brooks, up wooded hillsides, and finally down a quarter-mile long driveway, edged in granite pavers, and a low stone wall all engulfed in a canopy of trees. The road curves around the front of a magnificent mansion.

Not far from the mansion are the barns and buildings of the United States Equestrian Training Center (USETC), where many riders train for Olympic competition. The farm is very close to New York City and many large corporations have their headquarters nearby. We were selected to add golf to Hamilton Farm because of perceived environmental difficulties, problems that we are very, very good at solving. Thanks to a lot of hard work and dedication by our expert team of professionals, the permit phase was short and sweet.

We worked through a company called the Daylar Group. Harry and Jerry Day are successful golf course developers who offer project management and coordination for large development projects, so all a client has to do is to approve plans and pay bills. The Daylar Group does everything else, including selection of consultants, submittals for permits, solicitation of bids, clerking the works and even assembling publicity and membership packages.

The 18th green sits just below the terraced gardens of the mansion. The hole is a 431-yard par 4 that plays to a wide driving zone for average golfers that narrows for longer hitters. The second shot is slightly uphill to a huge green bisected by a nasty little front bunker. Hole locations on either the right or left are fun, but those behind the bunker are demanding. A closely-mown chipping area extends around the green to the terrace wall.

Most people's idea of New Jersey is not what is seen in this picture of the 5th green and 6th hole playing down to the barn. This area of north central New Jersey is a beautiful collage of rolling wooded hillsides, large estate farms and many valuable habitat areas. The golf course cohabitates on this land with the U.S. Equestrian Training Center. Between the two, a huge chunk of open space has been preserved.

This was a big project for a big client that could have a big impact on us if it turned out well. The plan was for 36 holes, a full-sized 18, The Highlands Course, and an 18-hole par 3, The Hickory Course. The actual clubhouse is a renovated sports center of nearly 20,000 square feet, and is elegant to say the least. It is located near the mansion, but is separate from it. The design of the big course had to provide returning nines near the mansion, keeping the USETC site intact and avoid wetlands, steep grades, rock outcroppings, horse trails, stone walls, turtle habitats and a bunch of other things. The par 3 course faced many of the same restrictions, except that each nine did not have to begin and end at the clubhouse.

This enormous project had many twists and turns and a fair amount of anxiety. Hurricane storms flooded parts of the land in 2000. It was a very wet spring in 2001. There were political squabbles and corporate intrigue. In the end, Hamilton Farm turned out great.

The 6th green sits within a few feet of an old barn that was part of the dairy known as Hamilton Farm. It was decided to preserve this remnant of the lands past heritage and incorporate it into the play of this hole and the par-3 7th in the distance. The barns have been restored for the maintenance center complex, storage and office space.

Dana, who visited the project on a weekly basis, developed a bunker style for Hamilton Farm that became the distinguishing feature of both courses. He patterned it after the bunker style of Alister MacKenzie, a splashy style found at Royal Melbourne and Kingston Heath in Australia, and Cypress Point in the United States. But Dana being Dana, he made the bunker faces steeper and deeper than the good doctor MacKenzie probably ever contemplated. The bunkers appear to be expensive to build and maintain, but these were the 1st bunkers to use a product called "Bunker Wol"®, a fiber underlayment intended to keep sand stabilized even on the steepest slopes. Other than Dana, everyone, including course superintendent Tim Christ, was skeptical that any material could keep sand from eroding off the near-vertical faces of Dana's bunkers. But after Hamilton Farm got 11 inches of rain from a hurricane, and the bunker faces didn't wash at all, the verdict was in. The bunkers at Hamilton Farm do indeed defy gravity. And fluid dynamics.

While some holes fit the land naturally, others, like the par-4 10th, require a massive amount of earthmoving to convert a steep hillside into a playable fairway. The amount of fill can be seen by looking at the left edge of the hole, but is not noticed by most golfers. Such earthmoving and shaping allowed Dana to establish play lines, strategy, sightlines, shot values, colors and textures. The correct blend all of these is an art.

Immediately behind the green on the downhill par-4 sixth is another set of old buildings worth mentioning, an old dairy barn and stables. The green is built so close to a wall of the barn that it could come into play when playing to some back hole locations. The inspiration for placing the green so close to the barn came from Musselburgh's Old Links, a grand old Scottish course my son Chris and I had played. Musselburgh's fourth green is hard against the wall of Mrs. Forman's Pub, which has a hatch door through which many a 19th century golfer could obtain a refreshment without leaving the course. There are no such trap doors at Hamilton Farm, but the barn wall still gets a fair amount of action. The adjacent stables, by the way, have been remodeled into offices for the superintendent and his staff.

From the first landing area, the par-5 9th is pretty spectacular. The building to the right is a restored and enlarged sports center that houses the golf shop, dining areas, locker rooms and offices instead of a swimming pool and tennis courts of prior decades. Short of the green (in the area between the bunkers) are two creeks, an island fairway, a pond, waterfalls, large trees, and 250 yards of air.

The freeform bunker style most often attributed to Dr. Alister MacKenzie has a ragged, organic look that seems more natural than more formal or geometric shapes. MacKenzie once described it as "looking like the last patches of melting snowdrifts." The par-5 14th would be dramatic with any bunker shape, but with the MacKenzie style, it is elevated to a much higher level.

The scale, depth and placement of bunkers doesn't follow any scripted formula or rules, and hence is the most free expression of a designer when defining play areas and shot values. On the 2nd hole, we decided to place a rather menacing bunker in the middle of the second landing area of this 568-yard par 5 to reward bold play over it and accurate play around it. It cannot be ignored.

Looking from behind the 7th green, you can see the barns and courtyard complex that is now the maintenance center. The exteriors of these barns were restored while the interiors are now high tech and efficient. The bull's barn back by the tee on this downhill par 3 has been converted into restrooms and storage. These barns are an important part of Hamilton Farm.

HOLE	PAR	YDS		HOLE	PAR	YDS
1	4	329		10	4	380
2	5	568		11	5	519
3	3	242		12	3	212
4	4	418		13	4	432
5	4	406		14	5	545
6	4	451		15	4	382
7	3	215		16	4	465
8	4	367		17	3	196
9	5	559		18	4	431
OUT	**36**	**3555**		**IN**	**36**	**3562**
				TOTAL	**72**	**7117**

HICKORY COURSE

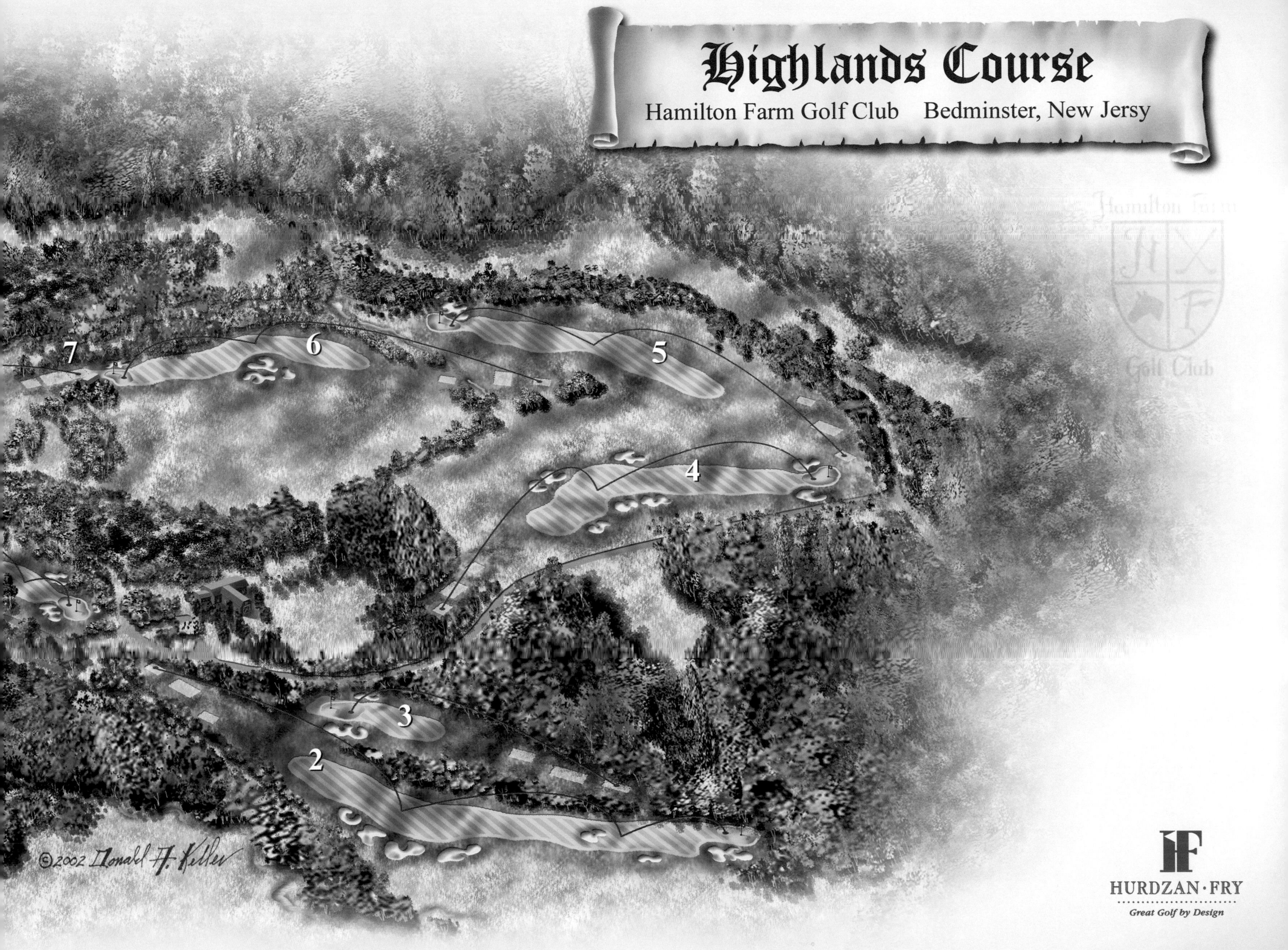

Highlands Course
Hamilton Farm Golf Club   Bedminster, New Jersy
Hamilton Farm
Golf Club
7
6
5
4
3
2
©2002 Donald F. Keller
HURDZAN·FRY
Great Golf by Design

It is often said that a well-routed golf course solves many site problems, and this is certainly true at Hamilton Farm, where we needed a linkage between holes that would be otherwise separated by a town water supply tank, a scenic buffer, a steep broad hillside, restraining property lines and 400 yards of distance. To make this connection, the par-3 3rd required very careful placement of features, limited tree clearing and some talented earthwork.

The 329-yard opening hole on the Highlands Course perfectly fits an open meadow that parallels the entrance drive just right of a very old stone wall. Only one or two trees were removed to fit in the green, and only a small amount of earthwork was required to cut a sightline through the front ridge. The existing mature trees provide most of the hazards. Bunkers are there only for definition.

There are many fine golf holes at Hamilton Farm, but none are better than the 18th, a long par 4 playing from a wooded bluff over a stream and directly toward the back side of the mansion. The 18th green, surrounded by tightly mown bent grass chipping areas, is set just below the mansion and its terraced flower gardens.

If there was ever a modern golf club that was inspired to duplicate the ambiance, grace and character of the great clubs of the Roaring Twenties, it is Hamilton Farm. It is one of Dana's all time favorite projects, a crown jewel of New Jersey golf. Nearly everyone who has seen the big course is baffled why it hasn't won every honor or recognition there is to give. Hopefully, someday it will take its rightful place among America's greatest golf courses.

◄ *The par-3 12th was purposely kept narrow to preserve as many of the trees as possible, as it borders several natural resource areas. To allow for good turf maintenance, the area under the trees was selectively thinned of unwanted vegetation and planted to shade-tolerant grasses.*

Sharply sloping hillsides usually make lousy green sites unless the designer is willing to make bold statements with earthmoving and shaping.

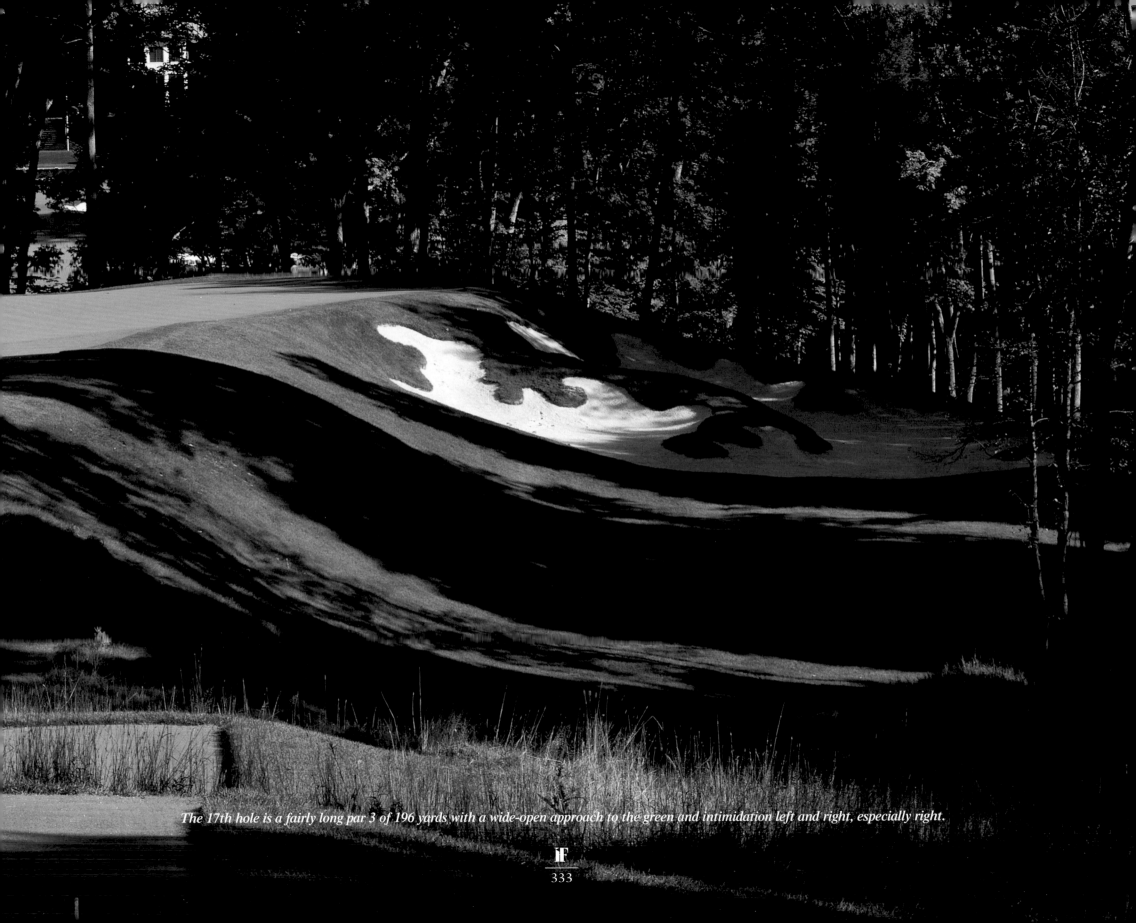

The 17th hole is a fairly long par 3 of 196 yards with a wide-open approach to the green and intimidation left and right, especially right.

Originally, the concept of the par-3 course at Hamilton Farm was for it to be played with antique hickory shaft clubs available in the golf shop. The idea was to establish a tradition where members and guests could experience the pleasure and pain of playing with clubs from the golden age of American golf (1910 - 1929), and on a short, less demanding course, so it would be pure fun. The greens and tees were to be designed exactly like those on the big, or Highlands Course but simply without the length of holes. The result is what some raters and critics are calling "the best par-3 course in the world."

The parcel of land that Dana and I had to work with could not have yielded full-length holes because of all the limitations we had. The site was bisected by a public road, a protected stream, and some of the most valuable wetlands on the farm. Then there were the problems that the available land had to allow for the USETC training and competition areas. The parcel was small and odd shaped, some development lots were required, the topography was steep, and the woods were mature and deserved to be protected. So the only way to integrate golf into the site was with par-3 holes.

If any picture is worth a thousand words, this picture of the 10th hole (and the 18th slightly right and above it) is worth millions. This was a historic pond that had become silted in and was permitted to be restored to its original shape and depth. The old barn structure is the irrigation pump house.

The site of the Hickory Course was blessed with many different types of managed-forest trees. Some holes are in softwood deciduous trees, others in hardwoods and holes like the 127-yard 12th are mostly in pines and spruces. This variety makes each hole distinct but visually related to other holes by a common bunker style.

Another key to designing a fabulous ➤ par 3 course is to give as much variety as possible in hole length, direction, topography, backdrops and shaping. The 218-yard 6th has low profile shaping and modest bunkering but plenty of room for error.

This rather long (218-yard) 14th is strongly reminiscent of its big brother Highlands Course. The target is quite wide and the right side bunker is more for containment of errant shots than strategy. The square tees and native grasses are also themes used on the Highlands Course.

The total maximum yardage of the course is 3,080 yards, with holes ranging in length from about 125 to 230 yards. Holes play uphill and downhill, over and beside ponds and wetlands, out in the open, in the trees, over deep ravines and gentle meadows to make each distinctly unique from its brothers and sisters. The thread that holds all of these pearls together is the bunkering - that wildly flowing, irregular, flashy bunkering such as MacKenzie is credited for at Royal Melbourne, Kingston Heath and Cypress Point. If it is the trademark look on the Highlands Course, it is even more so on the Hickory course, for who but Dana would have the audacity to build a par-3 course with that look.

I believe what makes the Hickory Course so much fun to play is the infinite variety of golf shots it demands of the golfers. It is not just the tee ball, which can range from a wedge to a driver for average golfers, but more over it is the second shot, be it a long breaking putt or a chip from the fringe, or trying to escape a deep undulating bunker. The demands on the short game are like no other short course you have played.

If the 2nd hole looks like a picture from Dr. Alister MacKenzie's 1920s book on golf architecture, then we've succeeded. If this course does not look like any par 3 course you've seen before, then we've succeeded. If you have been fortunate enough to play this course and you found it an exhilarating experience, then you have succeeded.

The nice thing about designing a par 3 course for very experienced and sophisticated club members is that so much of the site can be left in native plant materials. The 3rd hole shows how we maintain the tee and green, mow a walk path and let everything else become low maintenance. The building in the background is a shelter house and restroom.

Golf holes built from meadows are much broader in scope and are of similar shape. The 13th hole was cut down into the grade with the generated fill used to build the outsides of the bowls. Non-play areas were planted to fine fescues and native grass blends.

HOLE	PAR	YDS	HOLE	PAR	YDS
1	3	206	10	3	146
2	3	148	11	3	154
3	3	148	12	3	127
4	3	174	13	3	153
5	3	184	14	3	218
6	3	218	15	3	186
7	3	188	16	3	141
8	3	171	17	3	229
9	3	155	18	3	134
OUT	27	1592	IN	27	1488
			TOTAL 54		3080

Hickory Course

Hamilton Farm Golf Club   Bedminster, New Jersey

17

16

14

18

15

11

9

10

Hamilton Farm
Golf Club

HIGHLANDS COURSE

18

1

IF
HURDZAN · FRY
Great Golf by Design

Good par 3 holes like the 13th are fine tests of golf and a good way for all golfers to sharpen their playing skills. Meadow holes like this one often require a judgment of the influence of wind.

During the summer of 2001, Tiger Woods stopped by and played a few rounds of golf with his buddy Michael Jordan, an honorary member of the club. They loved the main golf course, but had just as much fun on the par-3 Hickory Course. In fact, I am told that they played the big brother Highlands Course once a day, and the Hickory Course twice a day because it was so much fun. I was also told that Tiger stayed a day or two longer than planned because they thought playing the Hickory Course would better prepare him for his next tournament. That is a compliment!

When working in steep hillsides such as the 171-yard 8th, great efforts must be made to grade in a green pad large enough to allow a reasonable margin of error by average golfers. To this end it is best to keep the hole short, and balance bunkering and the right hillside with a bail out to the left. Good players can still attack.

As Hamilton Farm starts to build its own unique traditions, perhaps the hickory shaft club idea will be resurrected and then the true genius and spirit of this awesome little course can be experienced.

◄ *The key to a great par 3 course is to produce each hole of such quality that it would be dramatic on any golf course. The 4th hole is one example, 174 yards of excitement.*

SILVERTHRONE, COLORADO

RAVEN
GOLF CLUB

The Raven Golf Club at Three Peaks awaits in the heart of the majestic Colorado Rocky Mountains. Designed in a collaborative effort by Tom Lehman, Dr. Michael Hurdzan and Dana Fry, the course compliments the stunning beauty of the Rockies. At every turn Mother Nature will stimulate your senses and fire your imagination with awe-inspiring vistas of snow-capped peaks, towering pines, mountain streams and wildflower meadows exploding in color. Our design goal was not to compete with this beauty, but rather to produce a comfortable, safe, friendly way to be immersed in it.

The Raven at Three Peaks offers an appealing blend of traditional and modern architectural design styles. From the Alister MacKenzie-style bunkers to the rolling contours of the emerald greens, each shot requires strategy. Ranging in yardage from 5,235 to 7,413, Raven presents a truly fair challenge for players of all skill levels. Because the golf course is at 9,000 feet above sea level, the growing season is short, so the entire golf course was sodded (even greens), using 110 acres of sod trucked in from as far away as Arizona.

From behind the 11th green, one can see the tees just to the right of the distant mountain peak on this double dogleg par 5.
The pond is also the irrigation source and is kept full by snowmelt diverted under deeded water rights to the property owners.

In addition to a world-class golf course blessed with magnificent panoramas of alpine splendor, The Raven offers a multitude of amenities and services along with this pledge: "To provide members and guests with the finest golf experience possible through a memorable and playable golf course, course maintenance standards that are tournament ready everyday, and sincere, animated and innovative guest service that anticipates every golfer's needs. Experience the ultimate. The Raven Golf Club at Three Peaks awaits your challenge."

Sometimes the interface between earth and sky so blends together in color and texture as to seem indivisible. The little stream in front of the 15th green was created to divert snowmelt into the irrigation lake. It was also on this green that Dana rolled in a birdie putt to win the Opening Day Skins Game against Tom Lehman (our co-designer), PGA Tour player Andrew Magee, the former world long-drive champion Brian Pavlec, and club pro Rick Fretland.

The 7th hole has all of the elements of a classic golf hole. The strategy off the tee on this 418-yard par 4 dogleg-left tempts you to play as close as possible to the cross bunkers seen in this photo. To bail out right means an approach shot several clubs longer and contending with a front greenside bunker. The green contours not only define shot values for various hole locations, they reward play from the more risky left side of the fairway by better accepting shots from the left.

Golfers read and sense the golf landscape with their eyes. The more interesting the collage of color, texture and height we can design into the landscape the more memorable that visual stimulation will be. The Raven is one of the most sensual golf courses we've ever done, and we attribute that to the awesome majesty of the high country, punctuated by vibrant green patches of perfectly manicured golf course turf. It is like playing golf in a kaleidoscope of colors and patterns.

One of most golfers' favorite holes is the downhill par-5 16th hole. From the moment you walk on the elevated tee to launch a drive until you walk off the green 601 yards and 150 feet below, your vision is filled with awesome views and changing patterns of color and light. It is like playing golf in a kaleidoscope.

Looking back 213 yards from the par-3 14th green shows that great views are a full 360°. The water hazard was originally a beaver pond enlarged and planted with wetland plants to naturalize its edges.

≺ *Looking backwards at the 1st hole gives one the sense of width and playability, with the strong and often unpredictable winds off the mountains to contend with. A generous fairway on the opening hole was given for a fair start.*

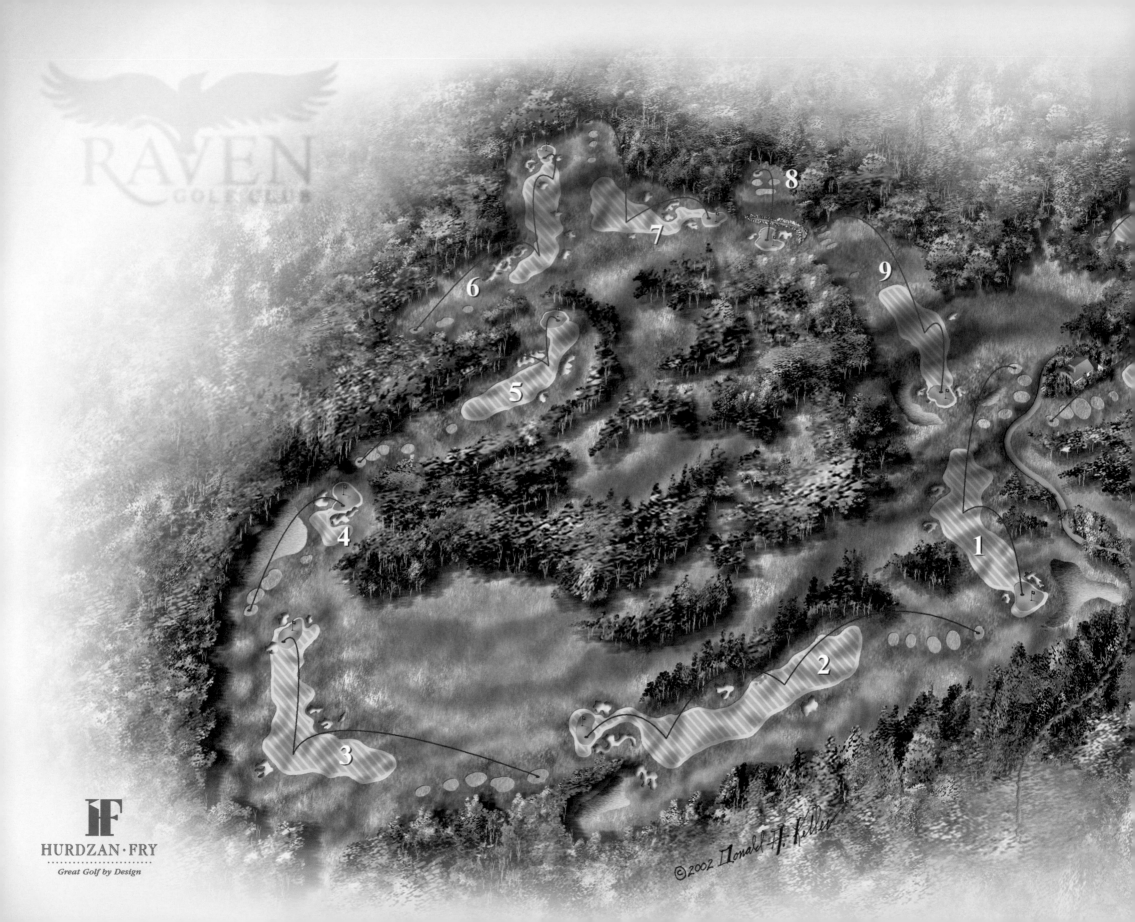

The Raven GC

at Three Peaks   Silverthorne, Colorado

HOLE	PAR	YDS	HOLE	PAR	YDS
1	4	426	10	4	367
2	5	587	11	5	599
3	4	450	12	3	237
4	3	164	13	4	434
5	4	345	14	3	213
6	5	543	15	4	415
7	4	418	16	5	601
8	3	184	17	4	468
9	4	514	18	4	448
OUT	36	3631	IN	36	3782
			TOTAL 72		7413

Mountain golf is an exhilarating experience of fresh cool air, thinned by altitude so shots go at least 10% further. Surprisingly, only about 4 or 5 inches of rain fall in the summer, so almost every day is a great golf day. However, some mornings you'll need to wait for the frost to give way to 80-degree daytime temperatures.

The routing yields to the mountain terrain and lies on natural plateaus formed by ancient landslides and weathering. The total contour interval change is 380 feet, and the maximum on one hole, (number 9) is a 200 foot drop from the tee to the landing area.

Where off-site views were less dramatic, we shifted the golfers' focus inward towards golf features. To maintain the level of visual excitement, we decided on a bunker style found at the MacKenzie courses at Cypress Point, Royal Melbourne, and Kingston Heath. These bunkers, with their organic shapes, seem to move in response to unseen forces, so that the landscape appears alive and vibrant. Less articulate shapes would be easier to maintain, but would appear lifeless. Clients made the final decision to accept higher maintenance cost in order to achieve a higher "wow" factor.

The par-4, 10th shows the concept of a wide driving area, defined by bunkers and tree lines, that narrows as one approaches the green. Although golfers prefer downhill holes, there must occasionally be uphill holes in the mountains. Notice how the MacKenzie-style bunkering fits naturally into the ruggedness of the site.

The Raven's panoramic views are so huge that a camera could only capture two of the three peaks for which the golf course is named. The 11th green is on the lower left and the 17th hole can be seen farther up.

Calusa Pines

When a man gets a second chance at life, he often seems to live life to the fullest. Chicago businessman and venture capitalist Gary Chensoff is such a man. After surviving a rare and often deadly form of cancer, Gary's philosophy was to play the remainder of his life from the very tips. That strongly influenced how Calusa Pines Golf Club was designed and built.

Before stricken with his illness, Gary considered our firm to design a 36-hole golf complex near Naples, Florida, after inspecting our accomplishments at Naples National, Sand Barrens and StoneWater, all of which were created from flat sites. Like many first-time clients, he hadn't heard much about us. He came to our office, met the staff, examined how we worked, called some past clients and thoroughly considered our qualifications and background.

On past projects, he'd chosen to work with celebrity designers whose marquees could help with marketing. We explained that we've never won a major championship and weren't the offspring of any famous family, so we were trying to earn name recognition through a history of diversely styled and successful golf courses. Gary asked, "If I hire you, can you produce a course that will be more unique than any other golf course in south Florida?"

"Sure," we said. "No problem." But privately, we wondered. Could we do the seemingly impossible? Every golf course site in south Florida has virtually the same characteristics -- flat, boring, densely vegetated ground highly regulated by all sorts of agencies. But we knew if any firm could come up with some fresh ideas, it would be us.

The first time the golfer gets to experience the huge ridgeline we created is off the 8th tee. The waste bunker zigs and zags all the way up the fairway before merging with the bunkers at the green. To the right and behind is more of the ridge complex, which at the far right corner boasts as the highest spot in Collier County, at an elevation of 58 feet above sea level. What is remarkable is the site existed at elevation 12 when we started.

We were blessed with a site that (for Florida) had an unusually deep ground water level of two feet. This meant we had two whole extra feet of soil to work with, crucial because most of Florida is extremely limited in how far you can dig down or build up. Gary made no requirement for housing, but suggested it would be nice if we found room for a few cottage sites. This complex was to have two completely different 18-hole courses, each with its own clubhouse, one being private and the other public.

To distinguish the site we decided to build several long sand ridges to meander through the golf courses. Both clubhouses would be located on a ridge top with holes playing down off and back to high points. The largest ridge would be built through a non-treed area on the private course and was designed to meander through several holes.

About the time we'd concluded our preliminary routings, Gary was diagnosed with a potentially deadly form of cancer. During the final permitting of the project, Gary underwent an operation and chemotherapy treatments. Always the optimist, he authorized the start of construction on the private course, even though he was uncertain of the outcome of his medical treatment. Things were humming along just fine, the contactor had pretty much completed the largest of the golf course fills, when Gary came out to the project, having beat the odds.

Always the opportunist, Dana suggested to him that the largest fill might look even better if it were just a couple of feet higher. Gary agreed. That was just the beginning of Dana pushing the limit, each time with Gary's blessing. Before it was all over, we'd created the highest elevation in Collier County, if not south Florida. It's 46 feet of fill, giving a finish elevation of 58 feet above sea level. The effect is incredibly dramatic. This "mountain" now influences golf on eight holes. Smaller fills along with a number of huge pine trees, give the other ten holes a special character.

It indirectly led to the name of the club. Gary had spent a lot of time studying the history and culture of the area, and visiting local points of interest. He was fascinated that the earliest inhabitants, the Calusa Indians, had built on Marco Island a fairly significant mound made of sand, conch shells and other materials. That prehistoric relic reminded Gary of our golf course fill, which in turn inspired him to come up with the name Calusa Pines.

This interesting view of the 4th hole requires some explanation. The bridge and the pier on the far right goes to an island that course owner Gary Chensoff built for his father to fish from. Sadly, his father died before the project was finished. The island now holds a brass cannon built by his dad that is used for all shotgun starts.

When the soils are well drained and the designer has some nice trees to work with, the concept is usually to do low profile earthwork and let trees and sand set the look and strategy. This classic approach, used on the 420-yard 1st, works best when integrated with contemporary shaping. These beautiful pines were one of the reasons that the name Calusa Pines was selected.

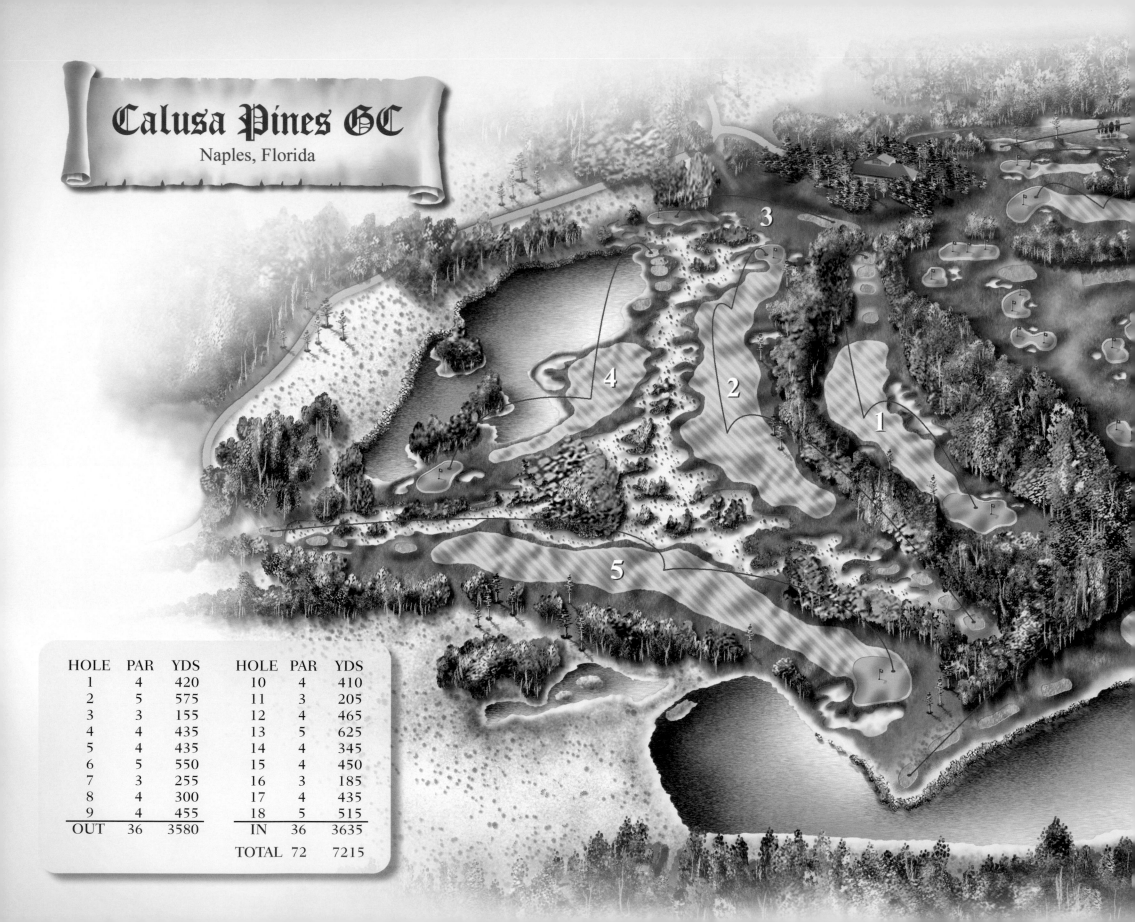

Calusa Pines GC

Naples, Florida

HOLE	PAR	YDS	HOLE	PAR	YDS
1	4	420	10	4	410
2	5	575	11	3	205
3	3	155	12	4	465
4	4	435	13	5	625
5	4	435	14	4	345
6	5	550	15	4	450
7	3	255	16	3	185
8	4	300	17	4	435
9	4	455	18	5	515
OUT	36	3580	IN	36	3635
			TOTAL	72	7215

Words can't describe the sensation you feel when you encounter the earthwork of such a huge scale at Calusa Pines. It doesn't look artificial. It looks believable. I guess there is some truth to the old saying that if you're going to tell a tale, tell a tall one, for there's a better chance it will be believed. One thing not exaggerated at Calusa Pines is it's wonderful, fun, laid-back atmosphere. Players enjoy a special brand of south Florida golf at Calusa Pines.

Low profile grading needs long slow changes in direction and elevation to avoid looking contrived. This 2nd hole is a 575-yard example, defined by nice stands of pines, tied together with sandy waste areas and punctuated with bunkers in strategic areas.

The view from the large earthwork that is the signature of Calusa Pines, provides a dramatic 185-yard shot that drops 40 feet on the par-3 16th. Various tees move to the left as they step down the hill giving easier lines of play. The huge oak tree by the green was transplanted to provide another unique look to an already good-looking hole. On the far shore is a pine strawed tree grove that is right of the 18th fairway.

Ground water levels may rise and fall as much as four feet from rainy to dry season. As a result, stream and lake banks are stone lined to look attractive during all seasons, others are treated with vegetation. Such lakes not only store water for irrigation, but they also separate holes like the 14th green (on the right) and the 6th green (on the left), as well as yield material needed to build features.

Trees in bunkers usually look strange, but not when in waste areas covered with native sand. The 7th is a very long par 3 of 255-yards, so the front of the green is wide open. Bunkers only come into play on the back hole locations, if you hit that far.

The area that separates the tee and the green on the par-3 3rd is a palmetto thicket and wetland. In order to see over the palmettos, the tee was raised about 15 feet and the green was raised about 8 feet. This thicket is home to many Floridians that run, fly, and crawl, but don't play golf.

From behind the 300-yard 8th is a good example of how waste bunkers work. The closer to the fairway the more maintained the waste bunker is. The farther from the fairway, the less maintained it is, until merged with dense planting and pine straw ground covering. Taller native and ornamental grasses are planted on some of the bunker noses for further accents.

How can I describe our reaction to being selected to add a second 18 to the Philadelphia Cricket Club? Thrilled, intimidated, concerned, challenged, fortunate and vindicated all come to mind. After all, our work would be adjacent to one of A.W. Tillinghast's masterpieces of golf course architecture. Comparisons between the master's work and ours will be inevitable. This is a world-famous club, with a history and tradition dating back to when golf was first established in America. This is a club where Tillinghast was a member, along with George C. Thomas Jr. (before he designed Riviera and Los Angeles Country Club). To become part of that legacy is good for our egos and our reputation.

Plus, the executive committee, board, members and staff of Philadelphia Cricket were highly professional, extremely patient, very understanding and some of the nicest people we have ever worked with. They treated us as old friends instead of hired help. The club president and golf committee were always involved, understood the problems and helped us find solutions.

One of the best ways to make a mandatory carry play fair is to place it between landing areas on short par 4's or longer par 5's. On the par-5 14th hole, a small stream and associated wetlands bisect the hole, with the second landing area on both sides, depending upon the golfer. The bunkers define major play areas.

One of the hardest things for a designer to do on a high profile project is to keep things simple. The 13th only has two bunkers, one cut in low in the fairway and a high-faced greenside bunker. The strategy is also simple: playing the downhill tee shot near the fairway bunker minimizes the threat of the greenside one.

And there were problems. We have collectively completed hundreds of projects in 35 states and around the world, but nowhere were the environmental regulators more ridiculous than on this project. For instance, the municipal engineer reviewed the plans and instructed us to exhaust our drainage pipes in an intermittent stream that flows through the property. But the Pennsylvania Department of Environmental Protection said we must exhaust the pipes 30 feet away from the creek into a grassy swale. It didn't make any difference to us which method we had to use. But each regulator wanted it their way. The local agency said to follow their guidelines or they'd shut the project down. Naturally, the state guys said if we didn't terminate the pipes according to their plan, then they'd shut us down. The two wouldn't or couldn't agree.

Philly Cricket already had a famous Tillinghast-designed golf course, and we knew that there would be comparisons between it and our new course. So we borrowed some Tillinghast trademarks, such as bunker placement and presentation, and incorporated them into a more contemporary look. The result can be seen on the 17th hole. Note how we used grassing and clearing lines to provide a visually striking but playable golf hole.

The new golf course abuts the old course in only a couple of places. One spot is where the new 3rd hole shares a quarry with the old 12th. The 3rd is a par 5 that can be reached in two by playing directly over the expanded irrigation lake. The quarry wall serves as a backdrop for the new green and plays as a side hazard to the old 12th hole above it.

The style of bunkering used on the 1st hole is reminiscent of the Tillinghast style used at San Francisco Golf Club. The bunkers have raised flowing edges with splashed sand faces to make them easily viewed on the landscape. The closer they are to the green, the more their faces are raised.

That's just one example of a dozen situations that were equally ludicrous. Thank goodness the golf committee members understood the absurdity of the process and were patient while things got sorted out. Before the project was completed, we had to obtain 42 separate permits. I personally saw this as a situation where small-time agency employees simply jumped at the chance to rake big time country club members over the coals for no real reason. There were no proven, or even theoretical benefits to the environment from their demands. It was simply a case where a group of employees used well-intended environmental protection laws as a means to obstruct open space development.

Enough complaining. I am pleased to say that the final result, the Militia Hill Course, is a beautiful test of golf, one worthy of comparison to Tillinghast's Flourtown course. Our design goal was to distinguish the new eighteen in a way that would complement the old course, but not clash with it. We used more tee boxes than found on the old course, but we kept the same square-edged shape as the old. Our greens are about the same size but their shapes are a little more articulated. Fairways are generally of the same nature, although ours might be a bit wider and perhaps better defined. As for our bunkers, we chose to use a more free-form Tillinghast style reminiscent of his San Francisco Golf Club, as opposed to the more oval bunkers he used at the Cricket Club.

Philadelphia Cricket Club

Militia Hill Course   Flourtown, Pennsylvania

1854

13

14

18

17

1

12

15

16

10

11

HURDZAN · FRY

Great Golf by Design

©2002 *Donald H. Keller*

2

8

6

7

9

5

3

4

TILLINGHAST COURSE

HOLE	PAR	YDS	HOLE	PAR	YDS
1	4	416	10	4	429
2	4	412	11	3	168
3	5	553	12	4	398
4	4	402	13	4	484
5	3	196	14	5	535
6	5	604	15	3	232
7	4	462	16	4	398
8	4	411	17	5	591
9	3	247	18	4	432
OUT	36	3703	IN	36	3667
			TOTAL	72	7370

⋏ The very long par-5 6th plays from the driving zone, to a second landing area over middle ground bunkers, then up a hill. The green is quite large and guarded in front by a small bunker. At 604 yards, this is a difficult hole for all golfers.

≺ One characteristic of both the old and new courses at Philadelphia Cricket Club is the placement of tees and greens so that holes play downhill on the drive and uphill to the green. On the 7th hole, a downhill drive should finish in the fairway across from the bunker, then it's uphill to the putting surface. The green could have been built in the hollow left of the green-side bunker, but it is much more attractive built as it is.

Square tees are coming back into fashion. But to use them yet provide enough variation in hole length and total teeing area requires some creative earthwork. The 11th hole has a total of five tees that actually add to the visual composition of the hole. Back and right tee locations bring the bunkers more into play than the left side and forward tees.

Militia Hill is still young, having opened in the spring of 2002, but already it has a sense of age and tradition. Like a fine wine, time will only sweeten the golf experience at Militia Hill. We're a little disappointed the project is done, because we made many good friends at Philadelphia Cricket Club. We will look forward to visiting them from time to time and, like old war buddies, reminiscing about the battles we fought together.

The original Cricket Club course has several holes that require ➤ *well-struck tee shots to reach the fairway. As the grading concept for the 12th hole was being developed, we decided to provide that same challenge by starting the fairway on a plateau beyond a valley in front of the tees. This makes for a very attractive downhill tee shot that rewards good play.*

IF

The 432-yard 18th hole begins with a downhill drive to a landing area, edged by a wetland, trees and a creek along the left and far end. The second shot is uphill to a green protected by two large bunkers. Not an easy hole, but it is easily remembered.